Street by Street

DERBY

BELPER, CASTLE DONINGTON, DUFFIELD, MICKLEOVER

Aston-on-Trent, Borrowash, Chellaston, Darley Abbey, Draycott, Findern, Kilburn, Melbourne, Ockbrook, Spondon

2nd edition November 2002

© Automobile Association Developments Limited 2002

Ordnance Survey® This product includes map data licensed from Ordnance Survey® with the permission of the Controller of Her Majesty's Stationery Office. © Crown copyright 2002. All rights reserved. Licence No: 399221.

Published by AA Publishing (a trading name of Automobile Association Developments Limited, whose registered office is Millstream, Maidenhead Road, Windsor, Berkshire SL4 5GD. Registered number 1878835).

The Post Office is a registered trademark of Post Office Ltd. in the UK and other countries.

Schools address data provided by Education Direct.

One-way street data provided by:

Tele Atlas © Tele Atlas N.V.

Mapping produced by the Cartographic Department of The Automobile Association. A01532

A CIP Catalogue record for this book is available from the British Library.

Printed by GRAFIASA S.A., Porto, Portugal

The contents of this atlas are believed to be correct at the time of the latest revision. However, the publishers cannot be held responsible for loss occasioned to any person acting or refraining from action as a result of any material in this atlas, nor for any errors, omissions or changes in such material. This does not affect your statutory rights. The publishers would welcome information to correct any errors or omissions and to keep this atlas up to date. Please write to Publishing, The Automobile Association, Fanum House (FH17), Basing View, Basingstoke, Hampshire, RG21 4EA.

Ref: ML084z

Key to map pages	ii-iii
Key to map symbols	iv-1
Enlarged scale pages	2-3
Street by Street	4-77
Index – towns & villages	78
Index – streets	79-91
Index – featured places	91-92

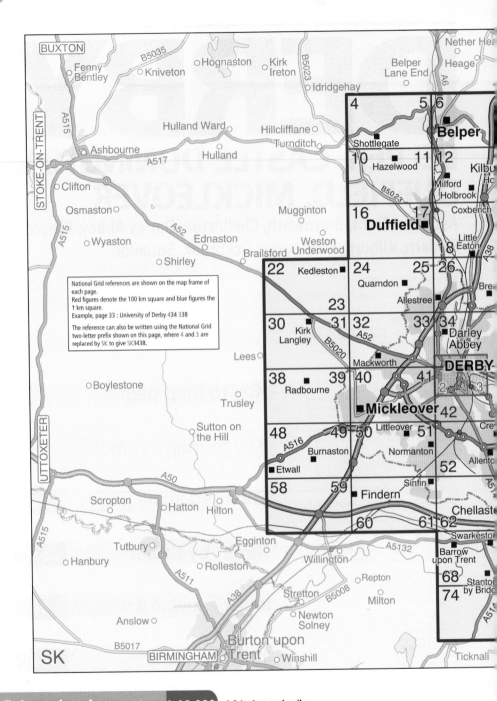

National Grid references are shown on the map frame of each page.
Red figures denote the 100 km square and blue figures the 1 km square.
Example, page 33 : University of Derby 434 338

The reference can also be written using the National Grid two-letter prefix shown on this page, where 4 and 3 are replaced by SK to give SK3438.

Enlarged scale pages 1:10,000 6.3 inches to 1 mile

0   1/4   miles   1/2

0   1/4   1/2   kilometres   3/4   1

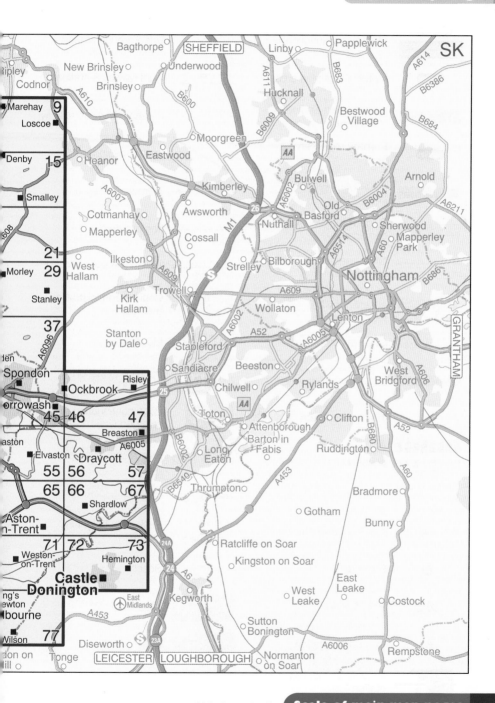

Junction 9	Motorway & junction	⊖	Underground station
Services	Motorway service area	⊖	Light railway & station
	Primary road single/dual carriageway	++++++++++	Preserved private railway
Services	Primary road service area	*LC*	Level crossing
	A road single/dual carriageway	•—•—•—•—•	Tramway
	B road single/dual carriageway	------------	Ferry route
	Other road single/dual carriageway	....	Airport runway
	Minor/private road, access may be restricted	- · - · - · -	County, administrative boundary
← ←	One-way street	ᵛᵛᵛᵛᵛᵛᵛᵛᵛᵛᵛ	Mounds
	Pedestrian area	**17**	Page continuation 1:15,000
============	Track or footpath	**3**	Page continuation to enlarged scale 1:10,000
████████	Road under construction		River/canal, lake, pier
⌐ - - = = ⌐	Road tunnel		Aqueduct, lock, weir
AA	AA Service Centre	465 ▲ Winter Hill	Peak (with height in metres)
P	Parking		Beach
P+🚌	Park & Ride		Woodland
🚌	Bus/coach station		Park
⇌	Railway & main railway station		Cemetery
⇌	Railway & minor railway station		Built-up area

	Featured building		Abbey, cathedral or priory
	City wall		Castle
A&E	Hospital with 24-hour A&E department		Historic house or building
PO	Post Office	Wakehurst Place NT	National Trust property
	Public library	M	Museum or art gallery
i	Tourist Information Centre		Roman antiquity
	Petrol station Major suppliers only		Ancient site, battlefield or monument
†	Church/chapel		Industrial interest
	Public toilets		Garden
	Toilet with disabled facilities		Arboretum
PH	Public house AA recommended		Farm or animal centre
	Restaurant AA inspected		Zoological or wildlife collection
	Theatre or performing arts centre		Bird collection
	Cinema		Nature reserve
	Golf course	V	Visitor or heritage centre
▲	Camping AA inspected		Country park
	Caravan Site AA inspected		Cave
	Camping & caravan site AA inspected		Windmill
	Theme park		Distillery, brewery or vineyard

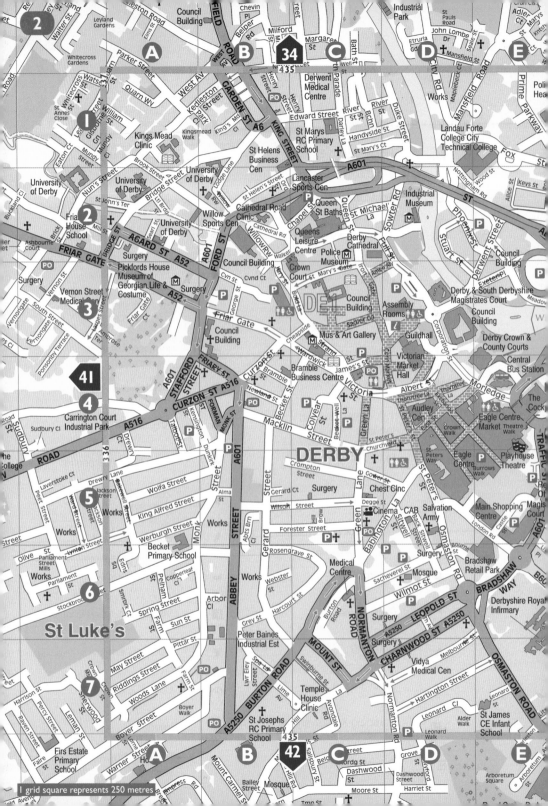

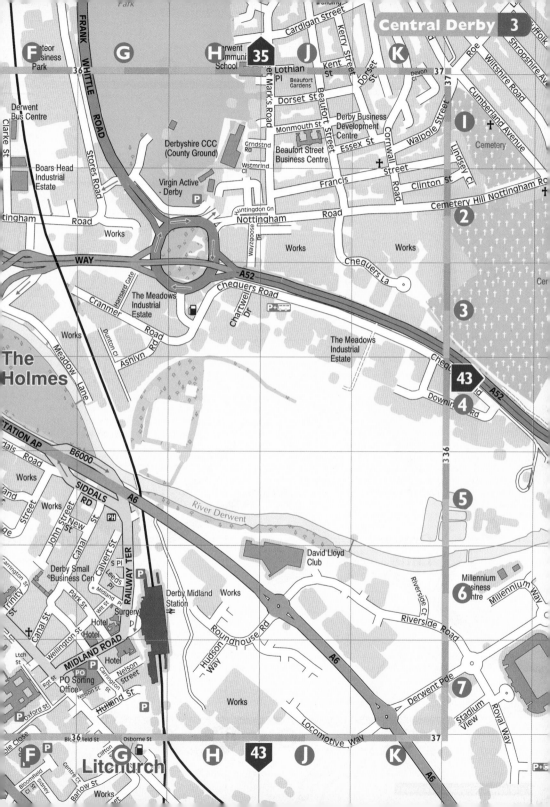

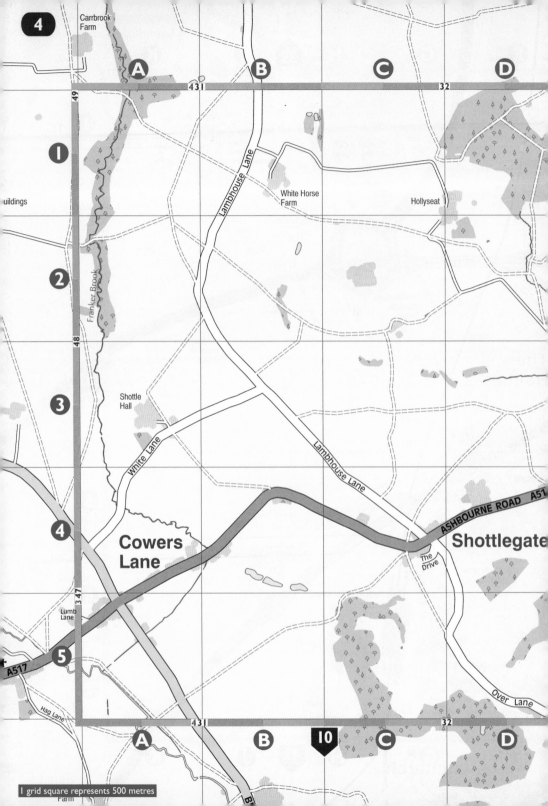

4

Carrbrook
Farm

A   431   **B**   **C**   32   **D**

49

1

uildings

White Horse
Farm

Hollyseat

Lambhouse Lane

48

Franker Brook

2

3

Shottle
Hall

White Lane

Lambhouse Lane

4

**Cowers
Lane**

ASHBOURNE ROAD A51

Shottlegate

347

The
Drive

Lumb
Lane

5

A517

Over Lane

Hag Lane

431

A   **B**   ▼**10**   **C**   32   **D**

B

Farm

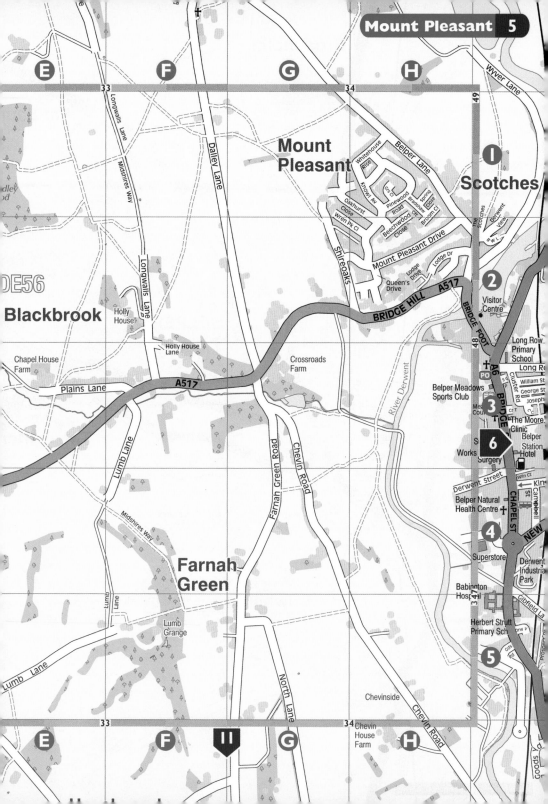

E F G H

Mount Pleasant

Longwalls Lane

Midshires Way

Dalley Lane

Belper Lane

Whitehouse Rise

Grn Ct

Knowl Av

Pinewood Road

Bradshaw

Spring Cl

Oakhurst Close

Beechwood Close

Wren Pk Cl

Broom Cl

Shireoaks

Mount Pleasant Drive

Lodge Drive

Lodge Dr

Queen's Drive

I

Scotches

The Scotches

Derwent View

S W l

2

Visitor Centre

DE56

Blackbrook

Longwalls Lane

Holly House

Chapel House Farm

Holly House Lane

Plains Lane

A517

BRIDGE HILL A517

River Derwent

Crossroads Farm

BRIDGE FOOT

A6

Long Row Primary School

Long Ro

PO

Cluster Rd

William St

George St

Joseph

Belper Meadows Sports Club

Mea Cour

3

The Moore Clinic

Belper Station Hotel

6

S Works

Surgery

Wiln Ct

Kin Campbel St

Lumb Lane

Midshires Way

Farnah Green Road

Chevin Road

Derwent Street

Belper Natural Health Centre

CHAPEL ST

NEW

4

Superstore

Derwent Industria Park

Farnah Green

Lumb Lane

Lumb Grange

Babington Hospital

Clotfield La

Herbert Strutt Primary Sch

prw V

Gos

5

Prospect Rd

North Lane

Chevinside

Chevin Road

Chevin House Farm

Goods

E F **II** G H

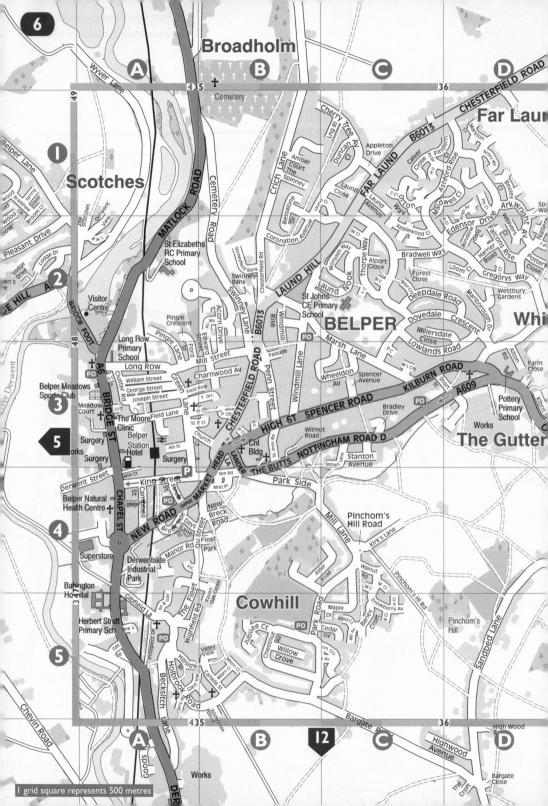

Boothgate

The Bent
Jackson's Lane

E   F   G   H

37   38   46
Street Lane

Iron Works Farm

Morley Park

I
Marehay Hall

Whitemoor Hall

Boothgate

Knob Farm

Morley Close

Morrell Wood Farm

Street Lane Primary School

2 treet

Whitemoor Lane

Hunter Road

Wicksteed Close

Scott Drive
Warwick Gdns
S Dr
B Cl
H Cl
Shrbr Dr
Morrell Wd Dr
Mrl Wd Dr
Hilary Cl
M Ct
Cook Close
Kndry Cl
John O'Gaunts Way
Royston Drive
Ashop Road
Crfn Wy
B Brd
Mtrln Cl

48
Street Lane

3

8

oor

St Jm Cl
Clwr CJ
Pytc Cl
LeChe Cft
Ash Acre
Burbage Close
Stoke Close
Beackden Cl
Yardley Way
Brafield Close
Over Lane

Belper Sports Centre

Ashton W
High
Cht Ct
Jodrell Avenue
Naseby Road
Royal Gate

Station Road

Park Hall Road

4

GATE

Openwoodgate

PO
KILBURN LANE

Openwood Rd

Ireton Houses

DERBY ROAD
47

PO
S
ster

Rykneld Hill

Rawson Green

Blackberry Way

Bramble Way
Blc Cl

John Flamsteed Comm School

5

Brookvale Rd
Brookvale Avenue
Brookvale Rise

Cinderhill

A609 BELPER ROAD

Hilltop Lane

Belper Rd

A38

Northfield Road
Brickyard Lane

WSON GREEN
13

Blackley

G

Works

Danesby Rise

Danesby Crescent

Denby Bottles

H

Prospect Road

NE

Bottlebrook Houses

E   F   G   H

37   38

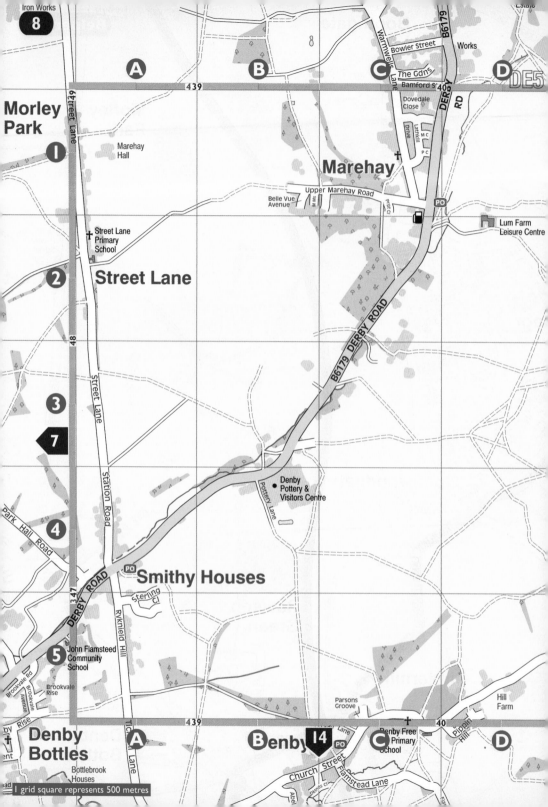

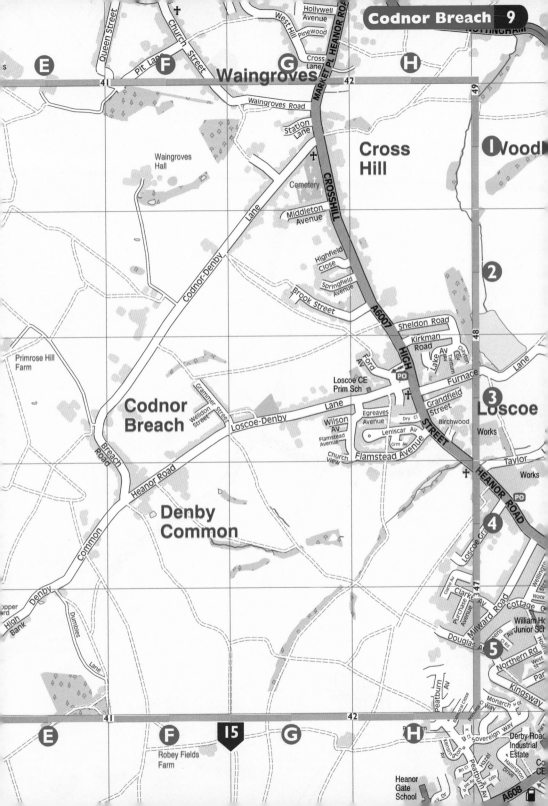

E F **5** G Chevinside **H**

Hazelwood

Lumb Lane

North Lane

Chevin Road

Chevin House Farm

I

Derwe Indust Estate

Goodwin's Lane

Hob Hill

Hazelwood Hill

Firestone

Spring Hollow

Hazelwood Hall Farm

Mitshires Way

Jacksons Lane

Chevin Road

Foun Lane

2

North Lane

3

Courthouse Farm

12

Sunny Hill

Wood La

45

Hazelwood Road

Golf Course

Mitshires Way

4

Hazelbrow

Moso Farm

Chevin Bank

The Oaks

Chevin Vale

Chevin Golf Club

Spring Hill

Golf Lane

Chevin Road

DERBY ROAD

Nether Close

Hazeldene Ct

Chadfield Rd

5

Centenary Way

Avenue Road

Lime Avenue

Riv

Cemetery

Castle Hill

E WIRKSWORTH ROA F **17** G **H**

Works

Phillips Croft

The Pastures

Holloway R

King Street

Vicarage La

Champion Ave

Castle Orch

ORD ROAD A6

William Gilbert Endowed Primary Sch

Duffield

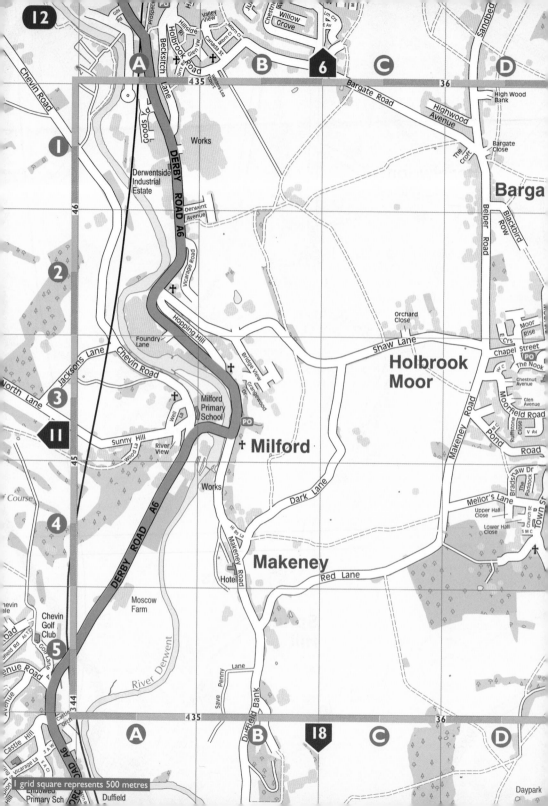

14 John Flamsteed Community School

Brookvale Rd
Brookvale Avenue
Brookvale Rise
SBY Rise

A

439

B

8 Parsons Groove

C

40

D

Pippin Hill

Denby Bottles

1

Bottlebrook Houses

Ticknall Lane

Denby

Lady Lane

PO

Denby Free CE Primary School

Church Street

Denby Lane

Abells

Okins Cl

Flamstead Lane

Flamstead

KILBURN

Edwards Crescent

Chapel Street

High Street

2

Bown Cl

Mayfield Av

Hillcrest Drive

Rowan Dr

Linden

The Chase

Windmill Av

The Walk

Elm Tree Av

Field Ct

Fairview Cl

Larch Road

Ryknield Road

Carr Farm

A609 WOODHOUSE ROAD

3

13

The Medical Centre

Ladylea Industrial Estate

Lady Lea Road

Golden Valley

The Crescent

C Rd

Chestnut Cl

Carr Fields

Fairfield Road

MAIN STREET

PO

Meadow Close

Calladine Lane

Cem

Hirst Farm

4

Golden Valley

Golden Valley

Horsley Woodhouse

Horsley Woodhouse Primary School

CHURCH LANE

A609

Stainsby Avenue

5

Lady Lea Hill

3 44

Wood Lane

Stair House

439

Golf Course

A Horsley Lodge Golf Club

B

20

C

40

D

Horsley Lodge

Woodside

| 1 grid square represents 500 metres

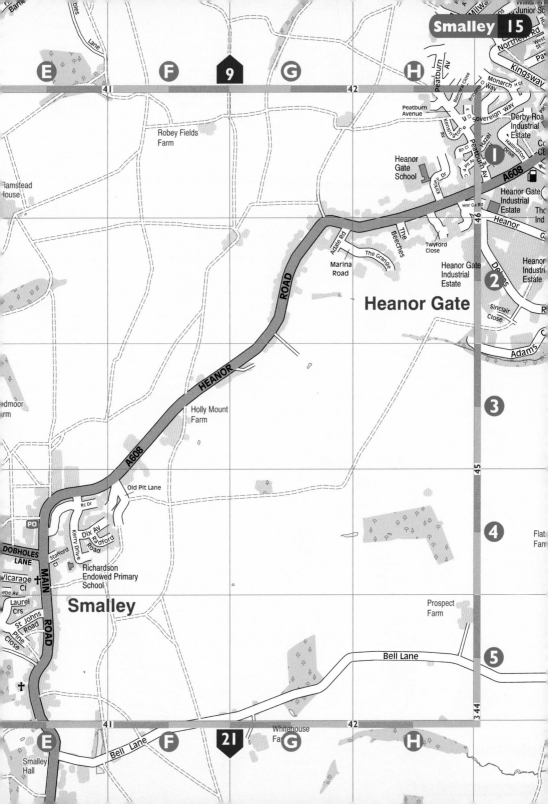

E 41 F 9 G 42 H

Bank
bles
Lane

MilWa

William St

Northumbe...

Junior Sc

West St

Pa

Kingsway

Peatburn
Av

Monarch H Cr
Way

Derby Roa
Industrial
Estate

Co
C

Peatburn
Avenue

Robey Fields
Farm

Flamstead
House

Sovereign Way

Heanor
Gate
School

Kirkley Dr

Bn Cl
Pt Av

Hnr Ga Rd

Adale Rd

Marina
Road

The Grange

The Beeches

Twyford
Close

Heanor Gate
Industrial
Estate

Heanor Gate

Heanor Gate
Industrial
Estate

Heanor
Industri
Estate

Sinclair
Close

Adams C

HEANOR ROAD

I

A608

Heanor

Derws

2

3

45

Holly Mount
Farm

A608

Old Pit Lane

Rc Dr

PO

Dix Av

Kerry Drive

Radford Road

Stafford Cl

DOBHOLES LANE

Vicarage Cl

ebe Av

Laurel Crs

St. Johns Road

Pine Close

MAIN ROAD

Richardson
Endowed Primary
School

Smalley

4

Flat
Farm

Prospect
Farm

Bell Lane

5

3 44

E 41 F 21 G 42 H

Bell Lane

Whitehouse
Fa

Smalley
Hall

16

The Clouds

Green Lane
Moseyley

A

Gun
Hills

Gunhills Lane

B

10

Windleyhill
Farm

C

Windley
Meadows

D

44

431

32

1

43

2

Newlands

Centenary Way

3

Cocks-
hut-hill

Woodfall Lane

Centenary Way

4

342

Hall
Close

Cu
Co

5

Ireton
Farm

edleston

A

431

Kedleston Road

B

24

C

Kedleston Road

D

Hay
Wood

1 grid square represents 500 metres

Spring
Hill

Centenary Way

E F 11 G H

33 34

WIRKSWORTH ROAD B5023

Works

Cemetery

Golf
Club

Nether
Close

Chevin Road

Chadfield Rd A519

Hazeldene C

Avenue Road

Lime Aven

Castle Hill

Castle
Torch

Milford Road A6

I

Duffield
Station

Phillips Croft

The
Pastures

Holloway Road

Champion Hill

King Street

Crown St

Vicarage La

William Gilbert
Endowed
Primary Sch

Snake Lane

Fisher La

Tamworth
Street

Old Mill
Close

The Meadows
Primary
School

Meadow Vale

Ferrer's Crs

Fairlawns

Broom

Park Road

Old Hall Av

Mll VW

Sp Dr

Hll Gv

DUFFIELD

Ecclesbourne
School

PO

Surgery

Ecclesbourne
Avenue

Surgery

2

Town Street

Wirksworth Road

Curzon
Lane

Devonshire Dr

New Zealand Lane

Cvn Cr

Scr Rd

M Cl

Granville

Melbourn
Close

Gilbert Crs

Hall Farm Road

Oak Cl

Chestnut
Close

St Roman's
Cl

Ecclesbourne Cl

St Roman's

Av A3

Centenary Way

Donald Hawk

Mak

McKenley Rd

Church Wk

3

Farnah House
Farm

Cumberhill
Farm

Cumberhills Road

Champion

BROADWAY B5023

Eaton
Ct

18

Broadway

4

Flaxhol

erhills
es

Cumberhills Road

A342

Burley
Meadows

5

Quarndon
Common

Quarndon
Hill

33 34

E F 25 G H

The Common

Coach
Drive

Montpeller

Burley
Drive

Burley
Grange

E F 13 G H

DERBY ROAD

French Lane

Coxbench Road

Port Way

B6179

Coxbench Road

Parkgate
Farm

38

44

Golf Course

Coxbench

The
Rockery

Horsley Lane

Coxbench Road

Sandy Lane

I

nalley Mill

2

Alfreton Road

Sandy Lane

43

Brackley Ga
Farm

Whittaker Lane

The Chase

3

Brackley

e

B6179

A38

The Leys

worth

n

Westley

rs

20

Moor Lane

Moor Lane

4

342

Drum Hill

*Breadsall
Moor*

Centenary Way

Morley Lane

5

37

37

38

E F 27 G

Hotel &
Country Club

H

Morley
Almshouses
Lane

Cen

20

A   B   **14**   C   D

Stain Hous

Wood ne

439   44   40

Golf Course

Horsley Lodge
Golf Club

Woodside

1

Horsley
Lodge

Smalley Mill Road

43

2

Sandy Lane

Woodside

Cloves Hill

Brackley Gate
Farm

A60

ILK

3

Brackley Gate

19

The Croft

4

Quarry Road

Morleymoor
Farm

Morley Hayes
Golf Club

342

Golf Cours

Bricklin Lane

5

Primrose
Drive

**Morley
Smithy**

A608

439   40

A   B   **28**   C   D

Morley
Almshouses
Lane

enary Way

1 grid square represents 500 metres

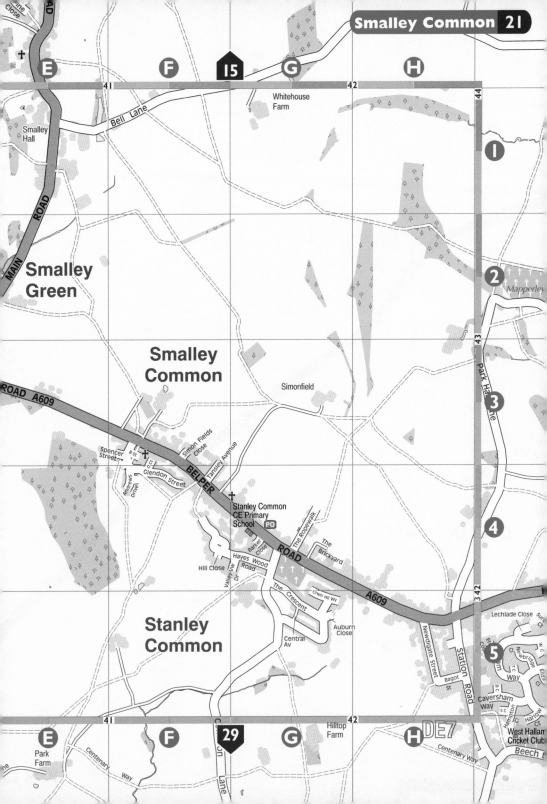

E   F   15   G   H

41   42   44

Bell Lane

Whitehouse Farm

Smalley Hall

Smalley Hall

I

MAIN ROAD

Smalley Green

2

Mapperley

Smalley Common

Simonfield

3

Park Hall Lane

ROAD A609

Spencer Street
B St
Simon Fields Close
Andrew's Drive
Glendon Street
BELPER
Tansley Avenue

43

Stanley Common CE Primary School
PO

4

The Ropewalk

The Brickyard

ROAD

Barker Close

Hayes Wood Road

Hill Close

Valley Vw Dr

42

A609

Stanley Common

The Crescent

Crwn Hill Wy

Auburn Close

Central Av

Newdigate Street

Station Road

Lechlade Close

5

Newbridge Way

Caversham Way

Harlow Ct

E   F   29   G   H DE7

41   42

Park Farm

Centenary Way

Hilltop Farm

Common Lane

West Hallam Cricket Club

Centenary Way

Beech

Cenetary Way

Ⓐ 427 Ⓑ Ⓒ 28 Ⓓ

Slade Lane

Wildpark

❶

Wood

❷

Wildpark Lane

Windy
Arbour

ASHBOURNE ROAD A52

❸

Snapes
Farm

Hilltop
Farm

The Burma Rd

The Burma Road

❹ Over Burrows

Nether
Burrows

❺

Kirk La

A52

Ⓐ 427 Ⓑ 30 Ⓒ 28 Ⓓ

Petty

Close

Ch

Flag

1 grid square represents 500 metres

E   F   G   H

29   30

Kedleston

Mercaston Lane

Moodersley

Buckhazels Lane

Lodge Lane

I

41

Wildpark Lane

Buck Hazels

2

Meynell Langley

Priestwood Farm

3

24

40

Meynell Langley

4

Lodge Lane

Lodge Farm

5

Flagshaw Lane

339

29   30

E   F   31   G   H

PO

The Cunnery

ley

Kirk Langley CE Primary

ASHBOURNE

24

A   B   16   C   D

431   32

Kedleston Road

*Hay
Wood*

edleston   1   Kedleston Road

Lane

41

2   *Kedleston
Park*   Kedleston Park
Golf Club

Golf Course

3

23

Kedleston
Hall (NT)

40

nell
gley

4   *Upper
Vicarwood*

5

339   *Lower
Vicarwood*

431   32

A   B   32   C   D

I grid square represents 500 metres

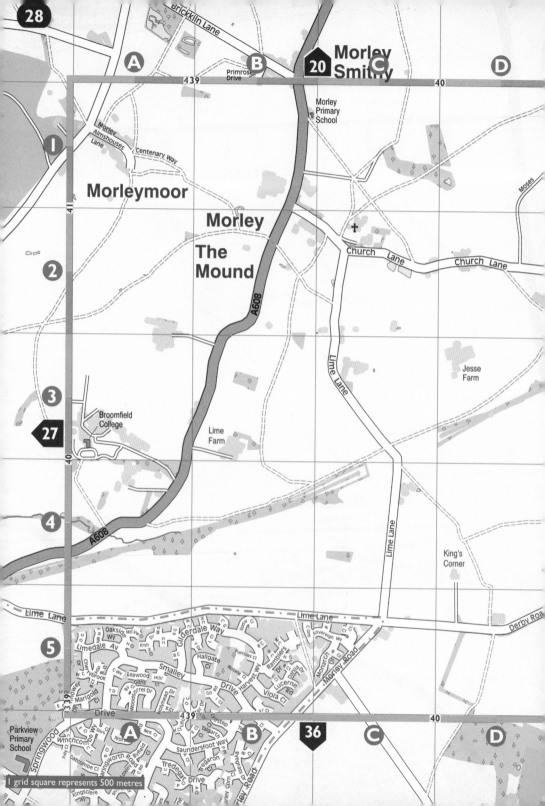

E   **F**   51   **G**   **H**

33   34

Sinfin **I**

Redwood Junior & Infant School

Sinfin Community School

Stenson Road

Stenson Fields

Stenson Fields Primary Sch

Grampian

Cobham

Nairn Cl

Tavistock

Pilgrims Rd

Monks

Quick Hill

Bluebell Rd

Bicester

Zetland Crs

Beaufort Road

Eggesford Rd

Holdernes

Blankney Cl

Derwent

Lundie

Trent

Wragley Way

Wragley Way

Sinfin Superstore

PO

Arleston La

Farmhouse

Osprey Cl

Ash Croft Primary School

Lauder

Dunbar

Melrose

Coltsfoot

Lomond Av

Deep Dale La

Road

2

Sinfin Central Busines

3

62

Arleston Lane

A50

Arleston Farm

A50

4

Trent & Mersey Canal

Merry Bower Farm

5

30

29

33   34

wyfor **E**   **F**   **G**   **H**

A5132

62

Lynwood
Montrose
Tiree Av
Links
Islay Road
Rona Rd
Iona
Maree Cl
Arran Cl
Redwood Road
Mead Cl
Myers
Sinfin Lane
The Chase
Haines Cl
Waltham
Hamblin Crs

A **B** **52** **C** **D**

435 36

Wilmore Rd

Redwood Junior & Infant School

Sin**I**n

Sinfin Community School

Sinfin Moor

Sinfin Moor Lane

Sinfin Moor Lane

Lea Farm

Farmhouse
Osprey Cl
Ash Croft Prim School
Coltsfoot Dr
Road
Cloverdale
Lomond
Deep Dale La
Sumatra
Leven Cl
Lauder Cl
Ettrick Dr
Hobkirk Dr
Jdbrgh Cl
Dunbar Cl
Melrose
Way
Watten
Loyne
Moy
Melfort Dr
Dunbar
Av

2

3

61

4

5

City of Derby
Derbyshire County

Sinfin Central Business Park

Moor Lane

Ashlea Farm

The Lowes Farm

Barrow-hill

Moor Lane

31
30
329

A **B** **68** **C** **D**

435 36

Sinfin La

SWARKEST

1 grid square represents 500 metres

Noel Baker
Community
School

Merrill
College

E **F** 53 **G** **H**

Shelton
Lock

Boulton
Moor **I**

Stourport Drive

2

Chellaston
Infant
School

Chellaston
Junior
School

3

Surgery

Chellaston **Chellaston** 64

David's Cl

Station Road

Chellaston
School

Cemetery

Glenwood
Road

Woodlands Lane

Boyd
Grove

Moyne
Gdns

Aston
Close

Walnut
Cl.

Ridgeway

4

5

Spring
Farm

A50

A514

A   B   **54**   C   D

439   40

A6(T)

Boulton
Moor

Stubble
Close

Thulston Fields
Farm

Shelsmoor Lane

Whtbn Dr
Lindfld Wy
Silverdale
Fellowlands Wy
Meltons Field
Orch Gdns
Pngtn Gr
Pinglehill Wy
Acrefield Way
Tuphall
Foxdell Chase
Low's Ct
Foxdell Way
3Acres Drive
Back
Lane
Sandyhill
Crw Dr
Netherside Dr
Fellow Lands Wy
Whitbourne Close
Pt Cls La
Chp La
Bensley
Cl
Tarlng
Cl
Cemetery

2

Marsh
Flatts

St
Gra
Willowbrook
Aston

Chellaston   Lane

A50

3
Chellaston

63

Aston
Lane

wdgr
T F Cl
Parklands Dr
Woodlands Lane

Chellas

4
Aston
Close
Ridgeway

Knob
Farm

Weston Fields Farm

5

ng

Chelia

329

439   40

A   B   **70**   C   D

Glebe Farm

E   F   **55**   G   H

Thurlestone
Grange

Bellington
Farm

I

31

Derby Road

Glebe
Farm

2

A50(T)

Manor
Farm

Fox Covert
Farm

Shardlow
Business
Park

A50(T)

Bird's Nest
Farm

3

Aston Hill

Alderslade
Cl

66

30

Hanger
Bank
Cem

Aston Hill
Farm

**Aston-
on-Trent**

Aston on Trent
Primary School

Moor Lane

4

Lane

Compton Avenue

Long Croft

Derby Road

Walnut Cl

Holden
Avenue

Green Leas

Clarkes
Lane

Road

Manor
Farm

Acre

Ellison
Avenue

Bell
Avenue

PO

Ash
Cl

Willow
Close

Valerie
Road

Posy Lane

Park View

shr pk

5

Weston
Rd

Willow Pk Wy

Rectory Gdns

Aston Drive

Hall Drive

Shardlow Road

3 29

Cft
Cft

Laurel

Holly
Ct

Maple Dr

E   F   **71**   G   H

Aston Lane

42

41

42

41

Aston Hall
Hospital

Trent & Mersey Canal

66

A   B   **56**   C   D

Bellington Hill

Ambaston Grange

Ambaston Lane

4 43   44

1

Bellington Farm

31

2

Glebe Farm

PO

London Road

Shardlow

Manor Farm

Clover Cl

Glenn Wy

Shardlow Business Park

The Grove Hospital

Alts Nook Wy

Shardlow Primary Sch

Wakelyn Cl

W End Drive

The Wharf

London Road

A50(T)

3

65

Cowlishaw Cl

30

Aston Lane

Trent and Mersey Canal

Canal Bank

4

Aston Lane

Roydon Hall Farm

A50(T)

5

Acre Lane

3 29

River Trent

Back Lane

4 43   44

A   B   **72**   C   D

Derbyshire County

Leicestershire County

I grid square represents 500 metres

Church
Wilne

E   F   **57**   G   H   S

45   46

River Derwent

Midshires Way

I

31

Great
Wilne

2

M1

Long Row

Lane

Midshires Way

Millfield

Work

3

Shardlow Marina
Caravan Park

B6540

Hemington
Fields House

Marina

River Trent

30

Cavendish
Bridge

London Road

PH

Donington
Lane

TAMWORTH ROAD

4

Netherfield Lane

A50(T)

Rycroft Road

5

Donington
Lane

Station Road

A50(T)

29

46

E   F   **73**   G   H

Willow Farm
Business

E   F   63   G   H

37   38   29

A514

I

Woodshop Lane

The Water Mdw

✝ **Swarkestone**

The Hall

2

28

SWARKESTONE BRIDGE

3

70

Swarkestone Boat Club

tanton y Bridge

A514

River Trent

4

3 27

✝

The Hills

Ward's Lane

A514

Ward's Lane

5

B587

37   38

E   F   75   G   H

Ward's Lane

Breach Lane

DE73

Main St   Main S

70

A   B   64   C   D

439   40

29

Glebe Farm

1

2

28

Trent & Mersey Canal

Hill
Farm

3

69

Park
Lane

P La

Main Street

Wilmot Av

Rectory
Farm

Trent & Mersey C

4

327

5

Ward's Lane

439   40

A   B   76   C   D

King's
Newton

Sleepy
Lane

Trent Lane

Main St

Hall Leys Lane

Main Street

Main

1 grid square represents 500 metres

E F 65 G H

Rectory Cl

Shardlow Road

Weston Road

Willow Pk

Aston Dr

Holly Ct

Laurel Dr

Maple Dr

Mulberry Wy

Aston Hall Hospital

Weston Grange

Trent & Mersey Canal

I

Weston-on-Trent

River Trent

2

28

Lane

King's Mill Lane

3

72

King's Mills

Hotel

Home Farm

4

River Trent

Donington Hall

27

5

Earthworks

E F 77 G H

Newton's Corner

County

72

A   4 43   **B**   **66**   *River Trent*   **C**   44   **D**

29

Derbyshire County

Leicestershire County

Back Lane

1

LC

28

Trent

River Trent

2

Short Lane

3

71

Walton Hl

Spittal

Hazeirigg

Campion Hill

Bentley Road

Shirley Cl

Darsway

Huntington

Haul Dr

Fox Road

Fosbrook Dr

Salter Cl

Staunton Cl

School Lane

Drive

Roby Lea

Queensway

Lan Pl

Orchard Primary Sch

Minton Rd

Grange Driv

Studbrook Close

The Green

Ferrers Close

Tipna Road

Cr Cl

Cordwell Cl

Kirkland Close

Orchard Avenue

Peartree

4

Park Lane

Paddock Cl

Bosworth

Starkie Avenue

Park Av

Park Lane

Road

Shields Crescent

Towles Pastures

Cheribough Road

Cooks Av

High Street

3 27

5

Crabtree Close

ton

ll Top rm

44

PH

Hill Top

Disew Road

A   4 43   **B**   **C**   **D**

1 grid square represents 500 metres

74

A   B   **68**   C   D

435   Ingleby Toft   36

1

26

2

Warsick Lane

Seven
Spouts
Farm

*Robin
Wood*

3

Knowle Hill
Farm

25

4

Woodside

5

3 24

Dame Catherine
✝ Harpur's School

✝

Chapel Street

A   B   C   D

STANTON HILL

Melbourne Lane

Bro

435

BURTON ROAD

Grange
Cl

Church La

A514

PO

Rose
La

Rose
La

Ingleby
La

MAIN   STREET   36

Banton's
Lane

Narrow Lane

STREET

Harpur
Avenue

Ticknall

I grid square represents 500 metres

E F **69** G H

37 38

B587

Ward's Lane

DE73

Breach Lane

Main St

Main S

PH

1

Netherfold CFS

Pack

Smith Av

Woodlands CI

Horse

DERBY ROAD

Melton Av

Windsor Av

The Woodlands

Oakla

2

Surg

Woodlands CI

Grange CI

Coronation Close

Queensway

Me J8

Acacia Drive

Spinney Hill

B CI

Rd CI

H CI

T C

Cft

Bloomw

Grange CI

Beech Av

Cockshut Lane Business Centre

Highfield House

MELBOURNE

Victoria Street

Derby

North St

South Street

Road

Chapel Street

Jubilee CI

Commerce Street

Hope St

Union St

George Street

Alma St

Dunnicliffe La

Branch Cft

3

Potter S

Church St

St Brides

Cockshut Lane

Riding Bank

B587

Selina St

Moira St

Quick CI

T C C

Main S

High Street

76

Washington Close

Ashby Road

Penn

Peniston Rise

Lane

Shaw House

ROBINSON'S HILL B587

4

Bleak House

Shepherd's Lane

Bog Lane

B587

5

Derby Hills House Farm

Woodhouses

37 38

324

E F G H Works

Stanton Harold Reservoir

A514

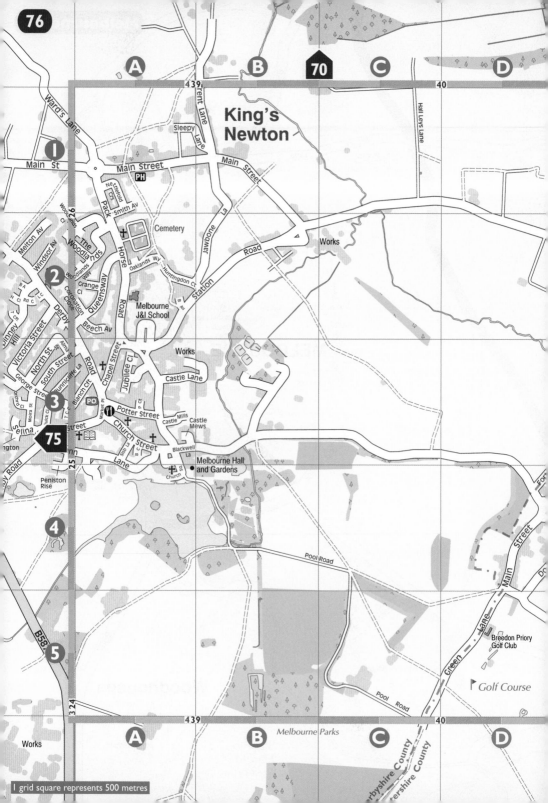

King's Newton

Melbourne Hall and Gardens

Melbourne Parks

Breedon Priory Golf Club

Golf Course

Derbyshire County
Leicestershire County

1 grid square represents 500 metres

Earthworks

E   F   **71**   G   H

41   42

Newton's
Corner

I

Derbyshire County
Leicestershire County

Donington Park
Motor Racing Circuit

26

Works

The Donington
Prix Collection

Exhibition
Centre

2

Ⓜ

Donington Park
Farm

▲ Donington
Park
Farmhouse

3   WALTON HILL

Wilson Hall
Farm

Slade Lane

Isley

✝ 25

Slade Lane

4

ilson

5

A453

3 24

41   42

E   F   G   H

MOOR LANE

Allenton	52 D5	Denby Common	9 F4	Langley Green	30 C2
Allestree	26 A5	Derby	2 C5	Lees	30 A4
Alvaston	54 A2	Draycott	56 C2	Litchurch	42 D3
Ambaston	55 H3	Drum Hill	19 G4	Little Chester	34 B4
Aston-on-Trent	65 G4	Duffield	17 H2	Little Eaton	18 D5
Bargate	12 D1	Duffieldbank	18 B1	Littleover	50 D1
Barrow upon Trent	68 B2	Eaton Hill	18 D4	Lower Kilburn	13 G3
Belper	6 C2	Egginton Common	58 B5	Mackworth	32 B4
Blackbrook	5 E2	Elvaston	55 F4	Makeney	12 B4
Borrowash	45 G4	Etwall	48 A5	Marehay	8 C1
Boulton	53 H3	Far Laund	6 D1	Markeaton	33 E3
Boulton Moor	63 H1	Farnah Green	5 F4	Melbourne	75 F3
Breadsall	27 F4	Findern	60 A2	Mickleover	40 A4
Breadsall Hilltop	35 E2	Flaxholme	18 A4	Milford	12 B3
Breaston	57 F1	Great Wilne	67 E2	Moravian Settlement	45 G2
Burnaston	49 E4	Gun Hills	10 A5	Morley	28 B2
Castle Donington	73 F5	The Gutter	6 D3	Morleymoor	28 A1
Cavendish Bridge	67 F4	Hazelwood	11 E1	Morley Park	7 H1
Chaddesden	35 G3	Heanor Gate	15 H2	Morley Smithy	20 C5
Chellaston	63 H3	Heatherton	50 C1	Mount Pleasant	5 G1
Cherrytree Hill	43 H1	Hemington	73 G2	Nether Burrows	22 A5
Church Wilne	57 E5	Hillcross	51 E2	Normanton	51 G2
Cinderhill	7 E5	Holbrook	13 E4	The Oaks	11 G4
Codnor Breach	9 F3	Holbrook Moor	12 C3	Oakwood	35 H2
Cowers Lane	4 A4	The Holmes	3 F4	Ockbrook	46 A1
Cowhill	6 B5	Horsley Woodhouse	14 B4	Openwoodgate	7 E4
Crewton	53 G1	Ingleby	68 B4	Osmaston	53 E2
Cross Hill	9 H1	Kedleston	23 H1	Park Nook	16 D5
Cumberhills Cottages	16 D4	Kilburn	13 H2	Pear Tree	52 B1
Dalbury	38 A5	King's Mills	71 F3	Pride Park	43 F2
Darley Abbey	34 B1	King's Newton	76 B1	Quarndon	25 F1
Denby	14 B1	Kirk Langley	30 D1	Quarndon Common	17 G5
Denby Bottles	13 H1	Langley Common	31 G3	Radbourne	38 C1

Rawson Green	7 G5
Risley	47 H2
Rose Hill	42 C4
St Luke's	41 H3
Scotches	5 H1
Shacklecross	46 A5
Shardlow	66 B2
Shelton Lock	63 E1
Shottlegate	4 D4
Sinfin	61 H1
Smalley	15 E5
Smalley Common	21 F3
Smalley Green	21 E2
Smithy Houses	8 A4
Spondon	45 F1
Spring Hill	11 G5
Stanley	29 H2
Stanley Common	21 F5
Stanton by Bridge	69 E4
Stenson	60 D4
Street Lane	8 A2
Sunny Hill	51 G4
Swarkestone	69 F1
Thulston	55 F5
Weston-on-Trent	71 E2
White Moor	6 D2
Wilson	77 E4
Windley	10 A3
Woodhouses	75 G5
Woodside	20 C1

USING THE STREET INDEX

Street names are listed alphabetically. Each street name is followed by its postal town or area locality, the Postcode District, the page number, and the reference to the square in which the name is found.

Standard index entries are shown as follows:

Abbeyfields CI *DERBYW* DE22........**34** B1

Street names and selected addresses not shown on the map due to scale restrictions are shown in the index with an asterisk:

Alwards Ct *DERBYSE* * DE24 ....**53** H3

GENERAL ABBREVIATIONS

ACC	ACCESS	CV	COVE	HRB	HARBOUR	ORCH	ORCHARD
ALY	ALLEY	CYN	CANYON	HTH	HEATH	OV	OVAL
AP	APPROACH	DEPT	DEPARTMENT	HTS	HEIGHTS	PAL	PALACE
AR	ARCADE	DL	DALE	HVN	HAVEN	PAS	PASSAGE
ASS	ASSOCIATION	DM	DAM	HWY	HIGHWAY	PAV	PAVILION
AV	AVENUE	DR	DRIVE	IMP	IMPERIAL	PDE	PARADE
BCH	BEACH	DRO	DROVE	IN	INLET	PH	PUBLIC HOUSE
BLDS	BUILDINGS	DRY	DRIVEWAY	IND EST	INDUSTRIAL ESTATE	PK	PARK
BND	BEND	DWGS	DWELLINGS	INF	INFIRMARY	PKWY	PARKWAY
BNK	BANK	E	EAST	INFO	INFORMATION	PL	PLACE
BR	BRIDGE	EMB	EMBANKMENT	INT	INTERCHANGE	PLN	PLAIN
BRK	BROOK	EMBY	EMBASSY	IS	ISLAND	PLNS	PLAINS
BTM	BOTTOM	ESP	ESPLANADE	JCT	JUNCTION	PLZ	PLAZA
BUS	BUSINESS	EST	ESTATE	JTY	JETTY	POL	POLICE STATION
BVD	BOULEVARD	EX	EXCHANGE	KG	KING	PR	PRINCE
BY	BYPASS	EXPY	EXPRESSWAY	KNL	KNOLL	PREC	PRECINCT
CATH	CATHEDRAL	EXT	EXTENSION	L	LAKE	PREP	PREPARATORY
CEM	CEMETERY	F/O	FLYOVER	LA	LANE	PRIM	PRIMARY
CEN	CENTRE	FC	FOOTBALL CLUB	LDG	LODGE	PROM	PROMENADE
CFT	CROFT	FK	FORK	LGT	LIGHT	PRS	PRINCESS
CH	CHURCH	FLD	FIELD	LK	LOCK	PRT	PORT
CHA	CHASE	FLDS	FIELDS	LKS	LAKES	PT	POINT
CHYD	CHURCHYARD	FLS	FALLS	LNDG	LANDING	PTH	PATH
CIR	CIRCLE	FLS	FLATS	LTL	LITTLE	PZ	PIAZZA
CIRC	CIRCUS	FM	FARM	LWR	LOWER	QD	QUADRANT
CL	CLOSE	FT	FORT	MAG	MAGISTRATE	QU	QUEEN
CLFS	CLIFFS	FWY	FREEWAY	MAN	MANSIONS	QY	QUAY
CMP	CAMP	FY	FERRY	MD	MEAD	R	RIVER
CNR	CORNER	GA	GATE	MDW	MEADOWS	RBT	ROUNDABOUT
CO	COUNTY	GAL	GALLERY	MEM	MEMORIAL	RD	ROAD
COLL	COLLEGE	GDN	GARDEN	MKT	MARKET	RDG	RIDGE
COM	COMMON	GDNS	GARDENS	MKTS	MARKETS	REP	REPUBLIC
COMM	COMMISSION	GLD	GLADE	ML	MALL	RES	RESERVOIR
CON	CONVENT	GLN	GLEN	ML	MILL	RFC	RUGBY FOOTBALL CLUB
COT	COTTAGE	GN	GREEN	MNR	MANOR	RI	RISE
COTS	COTTAGES	GND	GROUND	MS	MEWS	RP	RAMP
CP	CAPE	GRA	GRANGE	MSN	MISSION	RW	ROW
CPS	COPSE	GRG	GARAGE	MT	MOUNT	S	SOUTH
CR	CREEK	GT	GREAT	MTN	MOUNTAIN	SCH	SCHOOL
CREM	CREMATORIUM	GTWY	GATEWAY	MTS	MOUNTAINS	SE	SOUTH EAST
CRS	CRESCENT	GV	GROVE	MUS	MUSEUM	SER	SERVICE AREA
CSWY	CAUSEWAY	HGR	HIGHER	MWY	MOTORWAY	SH	SHORE
CT	COURT	HL	HILL	N	NORTH	SHOP	SHOPPING
CTRL	CENTRAL	HLS	HILLS	NE	NORTH EAST	SKWY	SKYWAY
CTS	COURTS	HO	HOUSE	NW	NORTH WEST	SMT	SUMMIT
CTYD	COURTYARD	HOL	HOLLOW	O/P	OVERPASS	SOC	SOCIETY
CUTT	CUTTINGS	HOSP	HOSPITAL	OFF	OFFICE	SP	SPUR

...PR	.........SPRING
...Q	.........SQUARE
...ST	.........STREET
...TN	.........STATION
...RM	.........STREAM
...RD	.........STRAND
...W	...SOUTH WEST
...DG	.........TRADING
...ER	.........TERRACE
THWY	.......THROUGHWAY
TNL	.........TUNNEL
TOLL	.........TOLLWAY
TPK	.........TURNPIKE
TR	.........TRACK
TRL	.........TRAIL
TWR	.........TOWER
U/P	.......UNDERPASS
UNI	.......UNIVERSITY
UPR	.........UPPER
V	.........VALE
VA	.........VALLEY
VIAD	.........VIADUCT
VIL	.........VILLA
VIS	.........VISTA
VLG	.........VILLAGE
VLS	.........VILLAS
VW	.........VIEW
W	.........WEST
WD	.........WOOD
WHF	.........WHARF
WK	.........WALK
WKS	.........WALKS
WLS	.........WELLS
WY	.........WAY
YD	.........YARD
YHA	.......YOUTH HOSTEL

POSTCODE TOWNS AND AREA ABBREVIATIONS

SHB	.........Ashbourne
PR/DUF	.....Belper/Duffield
WSH/BRSTN	...Borrowash/Breaston
DON/KEG	...Castle Donington/Kegworth
DERBY	.........Derby
DERBYE	.........Derby east
DERBYSE	.....Derby southeast
DERBYW	.........Derby west
HEANOR	.........Heanor
ILK	.........Ilkeston
LGEAT	.........Long Eaton
MCKLVR	.........Mickleover
MELB/CHEL	...Melbourne/Chellaston
NORM/LIT	...Normanton/Littleover
RDERBYSW	...Rural Derby southwest
RIPLEY	.........Ripley

Index - streets

Abb - Bar

A

bbeyfields Cl *DERBYW* DE22	34 B1
bbey Hl *DERBYW* DE22	26 C4
bbey Hill Rd *DERBYW* DE22	33 G1
bbey La *DERBYW* DE22	34 B2
bbey St *DERBYW* DE22	2 B6
bbey Yd *DERBYW* DE22	34 B2
bbot Cl *DERBYE* DE21	35 F1
bbots Barn Cl *DERBYW* DE22	2 B5
bells *RIPLEY* DE5	14 B1
berdare Cl *DERBYE* DE21	36 B1
bingdon St *DERBYSE* DE24	52 D1
bney Cl *MCKLVR* DE3	40 C4
cacia *MCKLVR* DE3	40 B5
cacia Dr *MELB/CHEL* DE73	75 H2
cton St *DERBYSE* DE24	32 C5
dale Rd *HEANOR* DE75	15 G2
dam's Rd *ASHB* DE6	31 F3
ddison Rd *DERBYSE* DE24	52 C1
delaide Cl *MCKLVR* DE3	40 B2
delphi Cl *NORM/LIT* DE23	50 D3
dler Cl *DERBY* DE1	34 C4
drian St *DERBYSE* DE24	53 E3
dwick Cl *MCKLVR* DE3	39 H4
gard St *DERBY* DE1	2 A2
imploy Ct *NORM/LIT* DE23	42 B5
inley Cl *DERBYSE* DE24	53 G2
insworth Dr *NORM/LIT* DE23	51 H2
lbany Rd *DERBYW* DE22	41 F2
lbemarle Rd *DERBYE* DE21	36 A5
lbert Crs *DERBYE* DE21	44 A2
lbert Rd *BWSH/BRSTN* DE72	57 H2
DERBYE DE21	43 H1
lbert St *BPR/DUF* DE56	6 A3
DERBY DE1	2 D4
lder Cl *DERBYE* DE21	35 F1
lderfen Cl *DERBYSE* DE24	63 E1
lderley Cl *DERBYE* DE21	35 H1
lder Rd *DERBYW* DE22	8 B4
ldersgate *DERBYW* DE22	32 C4
lderslade Cl	
BWSH/BRSTN DE72	65 G3
ldersley Cl *RDERBYSW* DE65	59 H3
lder Wk *NORM/LIT* DE23	2 D7
ldwych *DERBYW* DE22	32 D5
lexandra Gdns	
NORM/LIT DE23	42 C4
lexandre Cl *NORM/LIT* DE23	51 G3
lfred *BPR/DUF* DE56	13 H2
lfreton Rd *DERBYE* DE21	34 C3
lice St *DERBY* DE1	2 E2
lison Cl *DERBYE* DE21	35 G4
llan Av *NORM/LIT* DE23	50 B1
llen St *DERBYSE* DE24	53 E1
llestree Cl *DERBYSE* DE24	53 F1
llestree La *DERBYW* DE22	33 G1
llestree St *DERBYSE* DE24	53 F1
ll Saints Ct *MCKLVR* DE3	39 H5
lma Hts *MCKLVR* DE3	40 B5
lma Rd *DERBYW* DE22	2 B5
MELB/CHEL DE73	75 H4
lmond St *NORM/LIT* DE23	42 A4
lport Cl *BPR/DUF* DE56	6 C2
lsager Cl *DERBYE* DE21	35 H2
Alstonfield Dr *DERBYW* DE22	33 H2
Alton Cl *DERBYW* DE22	25 G5
Alton Rd *BPR/DUF* DE56	6 D3
Alts Nook Wy	
BWSH/BRSTN DE72	66 B3
Alum Cl *DERBYSE* DE24	54 B2
Alvaston St *DERBYSE* DE24	54 A1
Alverton Cl *MCKLVR* DE3	39 H5
Alward's Cl *DERBYSE* DE24	53 H3
Alwards St *DERBYSE* * DE24	53 H3
Ambaston La	
BWSH/BRSTN DE72	55 G4
Amber Ct *BPR/DUF* DE56	6 B1
Amberley Dr *DERBYSE* DE24	52 A4
Amber Rd *DERBYW* DE22	33 G2
Amber St *DERBYSE* DE24	52 D2
Ambervale Cl *NORM/LIT* DE23	50 D3
Ambrose Ter *DERBY* DE1	41 H1
Amen Aly *DERBY* DE1	2 C3
Amesbury La *DERBYE* DE21	35 F1
Amy St *DERBYW* DE22	41 H2
Anchor Fold *NORM/LIT* * DE23	42 B4
Anderson St *DERBYSE* DE24	53 G2
Andrew Cl *NORM/LIT* DE23	50 B1
Andrews Dr *ILK* DE7	21 F4
Anglers' La *DERBYE* DE21	44 D4
Anglesey St *DERBYE* DE21	35 E3
Anne Potter Cl	
BWSH/BRSTN DE72	46 A1
Anstey Ct *DERBYE* DE21	35 H2
Anthony Crs *DERBYSE* DE24	53 C3
Anthony Dr *DERBYSE* DE24	53 C3
Apiary Ga *CDON/KEG* DE74	73 E4
Appian Cl *BWSH/BRSTN* DE72	45 H5
Appian Wy *DERBYSE* DE24	54 C3
Appleby St *DERBYW* * DE22	42 A3
Applecross Ct *DERBYSE* DE24	61 H1
Appledore Dr *DERBYE* DE21	36 A2
Appledown Wy	
NORM/LIT DE23	50 D3
Applegate Cl *DERBYE* DE21	28 A5
Applemead Cl *DERBYE* DE21	35 F1
Appleton Cl *DERBYE* DE21	35 H4
Appleton Dr *BPR/DUF* DE56	6 C1
Appletree Cl	
BWSH/BRSTN DE72	45 H5
Applewood Cl *BPR/DUF* DE56	6 C2
Arbor Cl *DERBYW* DE22	2 B6
Arboretum Sq	
NORM/LIT * DE23	42 C3
Arboretum St *NORM/LIT* DE23	42 C3
Archer St *DERBYSE* DE24	43 F4
Arden Cl *NORM/LIT* DE23	41 H4
Ardleigh Cl *MCKLVR* DE3	50 A1
Argyle St *DERBYW* DE22	42 A3
Argyll Cl *DERBYE* DE21	45 E1
Arkwright Av *BPR/DUF* DE56	6 D1
Arkwright St *DERBYSE* DE24	52 D2
Arleston La *DERBYSE* DE24	61 G3
Arleston St *NORM/LIT* DE23	52 A1
Arlington Dr *DERBYSE* DE24	53 G3
Arlington Rd *NORM/LIT* DE23	41 G5
Armscote Cl *DERBYW* DE22	36 A1
Arnhem Ter *DERBYE* DE21	44 D3
Arnold St *DERBYE* DE21	41 G1
Arran Cl *DERBYSE* DE24	61 H1
Arridge Rd *DERBYE* DE21	35 G1
Arthur Hind Cl *DERBYE* DE21	34 A4
Arthur St *BWSH/BRSTN* DE72	56 C3
DERBY DE1	34 B4
Arundel Av *MCKLVR* DE3	40 C4
Arundel Dr *DERBYE* DE21	45 E1
Arundel St *DERBYW* DE22	41 G3
Ascot Dr *DERBYSE* DE24	53 E2
Ash Acre *BPR/DUF* DE56	7 E3
Ashbourne Ct *DERBYW* DE22	33 H5
Ashbourne Houses	
DERBYE * DE21	44 D2
Ashbourne Rd *ASHB* DE6	22 B3
BPR/DUF DE56	4 C4
Ashbrook Av	
BWSH/BRSTN DE72	45 H4
Ashbrook Cl *DERBYW* DE22	25 F5
Ashby Rd *MELB/CHEL* DE73	75 G4
Ashby St *DERBYSE* DE24	53 G2
Ash Cl *BWSH/BRSTN* DE72	65 G5
Ashcombe Gdns *DERBYE* DE21	36 A2
Ashcroft Cl *DERBYSE* DE24	54 A2
Ashdene Gdns *BPR/DUF* DE56	6 D2
Ashe Pl *NORM/LIT* DE23	42 A4
Ashfield Av *DERBYE* DE21	35 F3
Ashford Ri *BPR/DUF* DE56	6 C1
Ashgrove Ct *DERBYSE* DE24	36 A2
Ashleigh Dr *MELB/CHEL* DE73	63 G2
Ashleigh St *DERBYW* DE22	41 F1
Ashlyn Rd *DERBYE* DE21	3 G4
Ashmeadow	
BWSH/BRSTN DE72	45 G5
Ashop Rd *BPR/DUF* DE56	6 D2
Ashopton Av *NORM/LIT* DE23	52 A1
Ashover Cl *DERBYE* DE21	35 F3
Ashover Rd *DERBYW* DE22	33 G1
Ashton Cl *MCKLVR* DE3	39 H3
Ashton Wy *BPR/DUF* DE56	7 E3
Ashtree Av *DERBYSE* DE24	54 A2
Ash Tree Cl *BPR/DUF* DE56	11 H5
ILK DE7	21 F5
Ash View Cl *RDERBYSW* DE65	48 A5
Ashwater Cl *DERBYSE* DE24	62 A2
Ashworth Av *DERBYE* DE21	43 G1
Askerfield Av *DERBYW* DE22	25 F4
Aspen Dr *DERBYE* DE21	44 B2
Astlow Dr *BPR/DUF* DE56	6 C1
Aston Cl *MELB/CHEL* DE73	63 H4
Aston Hall Dr	
BWSH/BRSTN DE72	65 F5
Aston La *BWSH/BRSTN* DE72	65 H4
MELB/CHEL DE73	64 A3
Aston Rd *NORM/LIT* DE23	51 F4
Atchison Gdns *DERBYW* DE22	36 A4
Athlone Cl *DERBYE* DE21	35 E3
Athol Cl *DERBYSE* DE24	61 H5
Atlow Rd *DERBYE* DE21	35 F4
Attewell Cl *BWSH/BRSTN* DE72	57 E2
Attlebridge Cl *DERBYE* DE21	35 E3
Atworth Gv *NORM/LIT* DE23	50 C2
Auburn Cl *ILK* DE7	21 G5
Auckland Cl *MCKLVR* DE3	40 C3
Audrey Dr *DERBYE* DE21	35 H3
Augusta St *NORM/LIT* DE23	42 C4
Aults Cl *RDERBYSW* DE65	69 E1
Austen Av *NORM/LIT* DE23	51 E1
Austin Sq *NORM/LIT* DE23	52 A2
Autumn Gv *DERBYE* DE21	43 G1
The Avenue	
BWSH/BRSTN DE72	70 D2
DERBY DE1	2 D6
DERBYE DE21	43 G1
Avenue Rd *BPR/DUF* DE56	11 H5
Averham Cl *DERBYE* DE21	36 A2
Aviemore Wy *DERBYSE* DE24	51 H5
Avocet Cl *DERBYE* DE21	44 D3
Avon Cl *DERBYSE* DE24	61 G2
Avondale Rd *DERBYE* DE21	36 C5
NORM/LIT DE23	2 C7
Avonmouyh Dr *DERBYSE* DE24	53 F1
Avon St *DERBYSE* DE24	53 F1
Aycliffe Gdns *DERBYSE* DE24	53 G5
Aylesbury Av *DERBYE* DE21	35 G4
Ayr Cl *DERBYE* DE21	44 C2

B

Babbacombe Cl *DERBYSE* DE24	54 B2
Babington La *DERBY* DE1	2 C6
Back La *CDON/KEG* DE74	72 D1
MELB/CHEL DE73	63 H2
Back Sitwell St *DERBY* DE1	2 D5
Back Wyver La *BPR/DUF* DE56	6 A2
Badger Cl *DERBYE* DE21	37 E5
Bagot St *ILK* DE7	21 H5
Bagshaw St *DERBYSE* DE24	53 F1
Bailey St *NORM/LIT* DE23	42 A3
Bainbridge St *NORM/LIT* DE23	42 B3
Bains Dr *BWSH/BRSTN* DE72	46 A5
Bakeacre La *RDERBYSW* DE65	60 B1
Bakehouse La *BWSH/BRSTN* DE72	45 G1
Baker St *DERBYSE* DE24	53 G1
Bakewell Cl *MCKLVR* DE3	40 A3
Bakewell Dr *CDON/KEG* DE74	72 D5
Bakewell St *DERBYW* DE22	2 A5
Balaclava Rd *NORM/LIT* DE23	52 B2
Balfour Rd *NORM/LIT* DE23	52 B1
Ballards Wy *BWSH/BRSTN* DE72	46 A5
Ballater Cl *DERBYSE* DE24	51 H5
Balleny Cl *DERBYE* DE21	35 G1
Ball La *BWSH/BRSTN* DE72	55 H5
Balmoral Cl *HEANOR* DE75	15 H1
NORM/LIT DE23	41 E4
Balmoral Rd *BWSH/BRSTN* DE72	45 H5
Bamburgh Cl *DERBYE* DE21	44 C2
Bamford Av *NORM/LIT* DE23	41 H1
The Bancroft *RDERBYSW* DE65	48 A5
Bancroft Dr *DERBYW* DE22	25 F4
Bangor St *DERBYE* DE21	35 F3
Bank Ct *DERBYW* DE22	33 H3
Bank Field Dr *DERBYE* DE21	45 E2
Bankholmes Cl *DERBYSE* DE24	61 H2
Banksburn Cl *HEANOR* DE75	15 H1
Bank Side *DERBYW* DE22	33 H1
Bank View Rd *DERBYW* DE22	34 A3
Bannell's La *MCKLVR* DE3	49 E1
Bannels Av *NORM/LIT* DE23	51 E2
Barcheston Cl *DERBYE* DE21	36 A1
Barden Dr *DERBYW* DE22	34 A1
Bardsey Ct *DERBYE* DE21	28 A5
Bare La *BWSH/BRSTN* DE72	45 H1
Barf Cl *MCKLVR* DE3	40 B5
Bargate Cl *BPR/DUF* DE56	12 D1
Bargate Rd *BPR/DUF* DE56	6 C5
Barker Cl *ILK* DE7	21 G4
Barley Cl *DERBYE* DE21	18 D5
Barley Corn Cl *DERBYE* DE21	36 B1
Barley Cft *BPR/DUF* DE56	6 C5
MELB/CHEL DE73	63 G3
Barlow St *DERBY* DE1	42 B3
Barnard Rd *DERBYE* DE21	35 E2
Barn Cl *CDON/KEG* DE74	72 D4
DERBYW DE22	25 F2
RDERBYSW DE65	60 A2
Barnhill Gv *NORM/LIT* DE23	50 D2
Barnstaple Cl *DERBYE* DE21	35 H1
Barnwood Cl *MCKLVR* DE3	39 H4
Baron Cl *DERBYE* DE21	28 C5
Barrett St *DERBYSE* DE24	53 H2
Barrie Dr *DERBYSE* DE24	52 A4
Barrons Ct *BWSH/BRSTN* DE72	55 F4
Barron's Wy *BWSH/BRSTN* DE72	45 H5
The Barroon *CDON/KEG* DE74	73 E4
Barrow La *MELB/CHEL* DE73	68 D1
Barton Knowle *BPR/DUF* DE56	7 E3

Basildon Cl *DERBYSE* DE24 ....53 G4
Baslow Dr *DERBY* DE22 ....26 A5
Bassingham Cl *DERBYE* DE21 ....36 A2
Bass St *DERBY* DE22.....................33 G5
Bateman St *DERBY* DE1 ....42 D4
Bath Rd *MCKLVR* DE3 ....40 B4
Bath St *DERBY* DE1 ....34 B4
Baverstock Cl *MELB/CHEL* DE73 ....63 G1
Baxter Sq *NORM/LIT* DE23 ....52 A3
Bayleaf Crs *DERBYE* DE21 ....28 A5
Bayswater Cl *DERBY* DE22 ....32 C5
Beackden Cl *BPR/DUF* DE56 ....7 F3
Beamwood Cl *DERBYE* DE21 ....35 G2
Beardmore Cl *DERBYE* DE21 ....35 G1
Beatty St *DERBYSE* DE24 ....53 G1
Beaufort Gdns *DERBYE* DE21 ....3 J1
Beaufort Rd *DERBYSE* DE24 ....61 F2
Beaufort St *DERBYE* DE21 ....35 E3
Beaumaris Ct *DERBYE* DE21 ....45 E1
Beaumont Cl *DERBYE* DE21 ....34 A3
Beaurepaire Crs *BPR/DUF* DE56 ......6 C2
Beaureper Av *DERBYE* DE21 ....25 G5
Becher St *NORM/LIT* DE23 ....42 B5
Beckenham Wy *DERBYW* DE22 ....33 E5
Becket St *DERBY* DE1 ....2 B4
Becket Well La *DERBY* DE1...............2 C4
Beckitt Cl *DERBYSE* DE24 ....53 H1
Becksitch La *BPR/DUF* DE56 ....6 A4
Bedford St *DERBYW* DE22 ....41 G3
Bedford St *DERBYW* DE22 ....41 G3
Beech Av *BWSH/BRSTN* DE72 ....45 H3
   DERBYE DE24 ....54 A2
   DERBYW DE22.....................16 D5
   MELB/CHEL DE73 ....76 A2
Beech Cl *BPR/DUF* DE56 ....14 A2
Beech Ct *DERBYE* DE21 ....44 C1
Beechcroft *ILK* DE7 ....27 E4
Beech Dr *DERBYW* DE22 ....34 A3
   RDERBYSW DE65..................48 B5
   RDERBYSW DE65..................60 B3
The Beeches *HEANOR* DE75 ....15 H2
Beeches Av *DERBYE* DE21 ....14 C1
Beech Gdns *DERBYE* DE24 ....54 A2
Beechley Dr *DERBYE* DE21 ....36 A2
Beech Wk *NORM/LIT* DE23 ....41 G5
Beechwood Cl *BPR/DUF* DE56..........5 H2
Beechwood Crs *NORM/LIT* DE23......51 F1
Beeley Cl *BPR/DUF* DE56 ....6 D1
   DERBYW DE22 ....33 G1
Belfield Rd *RDERBYSW* DE65..........58 B1
Belfield Ter *RDERBYSW* * DE65.......58 B1
Belfry Cl *MCKLVR* DE3 ....40 C5
Belgrave Cl *BPR/DUF* DE56 ....6 C2
Belgrave St *NORM/LIT* DE23 ....42 B2
Bell Av *BWSH/BRSTN* DE72 ....65 F5
Belle Vue Av *RIPLEY* DE5 ....5 F5
Bellingham Ct *DERBYW* DE22 ....33 F1
Bell La *ILK* DE7 ....21 E4
Belmont Av *BWSH/BRSTN* DE72 .....57 H1
Belmont Dr *BWSH/BRSTN* DE72 .....45 G5
Belper La *BPR/DUF* DE56 ....5 H1
Belper Houses *DERBYE* * DE21 ......44 D3
Belper La *BPR/DUF* DE56 ....5 H1
Belper Rd *BPR/DUF* DE56 ....7 G5
   BPR/DUF DE56 ....12 D1
   DERBY DE4 ....34 A4
   ILK DE7 ....21 F4
Belsize Cl *DERBYW* DE22 ....32 C5
Belvedere Cl *MCKLVR* DE3 ....40 A3
Belvoir Cl *BWSH/BRSTN* DE72 ....57 F2
Belvoir St *NORM/LIT* DE23 ....42 A4
Bembridge Dr *DERBYSE* DE24 ....54 B4
Bemrose Rd *DERBYSE* DE24 ....53 F2
Benbow Av *MELB/CHEL* DE73 ....75 H2
Bendall Gn *NORM/LIT* DE23 ....51 F4
Benmore Cl *DERBYE* DE21 ....28 A5
Bennett St *DERBYSE* DE24 ....53 E4
Bensley Cl *MELB/CHEL* DE73 ....63 H3
Benson St *DERBYSE* DE24 ....53 F2
Bentley Rd *CDON/KEG* DE74 ....72 C3
Bentley St *DERBYSE* DE24 ....53 F3
Beresford Dr *DERBYE* DE21 ....44 D2
Berkeley Cl *NORM/LIT* DE23 ....51 G2
Berkshire St *DERBYE* DE21 ....35 E3
Bermuda Av *DERBYE* DE21 ....26 D2
Berry Park Cl *DERBYW* DE22 ....33 H2
Berwick Av *DERBY* DE24 ....34 D4
Berwick Cl *DERBYSE* DE24 ....54 A4
Berwick Dr *DERBYSE* DE24 ....54 A4
Bessalone Dr *BPR/DUF* DE56...........6 B2
Besthorpe Cl *DERBYE* DE21 ....36 A2
Bethulie Rd *NORM/LIT* DE23 ....52 B1
Beverley St *DERBYSE* DE24 ....53 E2
Bewdley Cl *MELB/CHEL* DE73 ....63 H1
Bicester Av *DERBYSE* DE24 ....61 F2
Bickley Moss *DERBYE* DE21 ....36 A2
Bideford Dr *NORM/LIT* DE23 ....51 G4
The Biggin *CDON/KEG* DE74............73 E4
Bilberry Cl *DERBYE* DE21 ....35 G2

Bingham St *DERBYSE* DE24 ....53 F3
Binscombe La *DERBYE* DE21 ....27 G5
Birch Cl *DERBYSE* DE24 ....37 F5
Birches Rd *DERBYW* DE22 ....25 G5
Birchfield Cl *MELB/CHEL* DE73........63 G2
Birchover Ri *DERBYE* DE21 ....35 G2
Birchover Wy *DERBYW* DE22 ....33 G2
Birchview Cl *BPR/DUF* DE56 ....6 C5
Birchwood *HEANOR* DE75 ....9 H3
Birchwood Av *NORM/LIT* DE23 ....51 G3
Birdcage Wk *DERBYW* DE22 ....32 C5
Birdwood St *NORM/LIT* DE23 ....42 A5
Birkdale Cl *MCKLVR* DE3 ....40 C4
Biscay Ct *DERBYE* DE21 ....36 B1
Bishops Cl *MELB/CHEL* DE73 ....76 A3
Bishop's Dr *DERBYE* DE21 ....35 F1
Blaby Cl *NORM/LIT* DE23 ....51 G3
Blackberry Rw *BPR/DUF* DE56 ....7 G5
Blackbird Rw *BPR/DUF* DE56..........12 D1
Blackmore St *NORM/LIT* DE23 ....52 A2
Blackmount Ct *DERBYSE* DE24 ....61 G1
Blackthorn Cl *DERBYE* DE21 ....35 F1
   MELB/CHEL DE73.................75 H3
Blackthorne Cl *BPR/DUF* DE56 ....7 G5
Blackwell La *MELB/CHEL* DE73 ....76 A3
Blagreaves Av *NORM/LIT* DE23 ......51 F4
Blagreaves La *NORM/LIT* DE23 ....51 F4
Blakebrook Dr *MELB/CHEL* DE73.....63 H1
Blakeley La *RDERBYSW* DE65.........58 A1
Blakelow Dr *RDERBYSW* DE65........58 A1
Blakemore Av *MELB/CHEL* DE73.....76 A2
Blanch Cft *MELB/CHEL* DE73 ....76 A3
Blandford Cl *DERBYSE* DE24 ....54 C3
Blankney Cl *DERBYE* DE21 ....61 G2
Blencathra Dr *MCKLVR* DE3 ....50 B1
Blenheim Cl *BPR/DUF* DE56.............7 E2
Blenheim Dr *DERBYW* DE22 ....25 F5
Blenheim Ms *RDERBYSW* * DE65.....48 B5
Blenheim Pde *DERBYW* DE22 ....25 H4
Blind La *BWSH/BRSTN* DE72 ....57 G1
Blithfield Gdns *MELB/CHEL* DE73....63 H2
Bloomfield Cl *DERBYE* DE21 ....42 C3
Bloomfield St *DERBY* DE1 ....42 C3
Bluebell Cl *DERBYSE* DE24 ....61 F2
Bluebird St *DERBYSE* DE24 ....51 G5
Blunt St *ILK* DE7 ....21 F3
Blyth Pl *DERBYE* DE21 ....35 E2
Boden St *NORM/LIT* DE23 ....42 C4
Bodmin Cl *DERBYSE* DE24 ....61 G1
Bog La *MELB/CHEL* DE73 ....75 F5
Bold La *DERBY* DE1 ....2 C3
Bonchurch Cl *DERBYSE* DE24 ....54 B4
Bondgate *CDON/KEG* DE74 ....73 E4
Bonnie Prince Charlie Wk
   DERBYW DE22.....................32 B5
Bonnyrigg Dr *DERBYE* DE21 ....35 H1
Bonsall Av *NORM/LIT* DE23 ....51 G1
Bonsall Dr *MCKLVR* DE3 ....40 B3
Boothgate *BPR/DUF* DE56 ....7 F1
Booth St *DERBYSE* DE24 ....53 G2
Border Crs *DERBYSE* DE24 ....54 A5
Borough St *CDON/KEG* DE74 ....73 E4
Borrowash By-Pass
   DERBYE DE21 ....44 A3
Borrowash Rd *DERBYE* DE21 ....45 E3
Borrowfield Rd *DERBYE* DE21 ....44 D3
Borrowfields
   BWSH/BRSTN DE72...............45 G5
Boscastle Cl *DERBYSE* DE24 ....54 A3
Boston Cl *DERBYE* DE21 ....36 B5
Boswell Sq *NORM/LIT* DE23 ....52 A2
Bosworth Av *NORM/LIT* DE23 ....51 H3
Bosworth Rd *CDON/KEG* DE74 ....72 C4
Boulton Dr *DERBYSE* DE24 ....53 H3
Boulton La *DERBYSE* DE24 ....53 G4
Boundary Rd *DERBYW* DE22 ....41 H2
   RDERBYSW DE65..................58 C4
Bourne Sq *BWSH/BRSTN* DE72.......57 H1
Bourne St *DERBY* DE1 ....2 D6
Bowbank Cl *NORM/LIT* DE23 ....50 D3
Bowbridge Av *NORM/LIT* DE23 ....51 F4
Bower St *DERBYSE* DE24 ....53 G1
Bowland Cl *MCKLVR* DE3 ....40 B5
Bowlees Ct *NORM/LIT* DE23 ....50 B2
Bowler Dr *BPR/DUF* DE56 ....13 H3
Bowmer Rd *DERBYSE* DE24 ....43 F5
Bown Cl *BPR/DUF* DE56 ....13 H2
Boxmoor Cl *NORM/LIT* DE23 ....50 C2
Boyd Gv *MELB/CHEL* DE73 ....63 H4
Boyer St *DERBY* DE22 ....41 H3
Boyer Wk *DERBY* DE22 ....2 A7
Boylestone Rd *NORM/LIT* DE23 ......51 F4
Brackens Av *DERBYE* DE21 ....53 G3
Brackensdale Av *DERBYW* DE22.....41 E1
Bracken's La *DERBYE* DE21 ....53 G3
Brackley *BPR/DUF* DE56 ....13 G1
Brackley Dr *DERBYE* DE21 ....44 D1

Brackley Ga *ILK* DE7 ....19 H3
Bracknell Dr *DERBYSE* DE24..........53 H4
Bradbourne St *DERBYW* * DE22 .....41 H3
Bradbury Cl *BWSH/BRSTN* DE72 ....45 H5
Bradgate Ct *NORM/LIT* DE23 ....51 H3
Brading Cl *DERBYE* DE24 ....54 C4
Bradley Dr *BPR/DUF* DE56 ....6 A4
Bradley St *DERBYW* DE22 ....33 H3
Bradmoor Gv *MELB/CHEL* DE73 .....64 A2
Bradshaw Cft *BPR/DUF* DE56 ....5 H1
Bradshaw Dr *BPR/DUF* DE56 ....12 D4
Bradshaw Wy *DERBY* DE1 ....2 E6
Bradwell Cl *MCKLVR* DE3 ....40 B5
Bradwell Wy *BPR/DUF* DE56 ....6 C2
Braemar Cl *DERBYSE* DE24 ....61 G1
Brafield Cl *BPR/DUF* DE56 ....7 E3
Brailsford Rd *DERBYE* DE21 ....35 F3
Braintree Cl *DERBYE* DE21.............28 A5
Braithwell Cl *DERBYW* DE22 ....34 A1
Bramberry Cl *DERBYE* DE21...........28 A5
Bramble Ms *MCKLVR* DE3 ....40 A5
Bramble St *DERBY* DE1 ....2 B6
Bramble Wy *BPR/DUF* DE56 ....7 G5
Bramblewick Dr *NORM/LIT* DE23.....50 D3
Brambling Gdns *MCKLVR* DE3.........49 F2
Bramfield Av *DERBYW* DE22 ....33 F1
Bramley Cl *DERBYE* DE21 ....28 B5
Brampton Cl *MCKLVR* DE3 ....39 H3
Brampton Ct *BPR/DUF* * DE56 ....7 E3
Brandelhow Ct *DERBYE* DE21.........28 A5
Branksome Av *DERBYE* DE24 ....54 B2
Brassington Rd *DERBYE* DE21.........35 G2
Brayfield Av *NORM/LIT* DE23 ....51 G1
Brayfield Rd *NORM/LIT* DE23 ....51 F1
Breach La *MELB/CHEL* DE73 ....75 F1
Breach Rd *RIPLEY* DE5 ....9 E3
Breaston La *BWSH/BRSTN* DE72 ....47 G2
Brecon Cl *DERBYE* DE21 ....36 D5
Breedon Av *NORM/LIT* DE23 ....51 G4
Breedon Hill Rd *NORM/LIT* DE23.....42 A3
Brentford Dr *DERBYW* DE22 ....33 E3
Bretby Sq *NORM/LIT* DE23 ....51 F4
Bretton Av *NORM/LIT* DE23 ....41 F4
Bretton Rd *BPR/DUF* DE56 ....7 F2
Breydon Cl *DERBYSE* DE24 ....54 B3
Briar Cl *BWSH/BRSTN* DE72 ....45 H5
   DERBYE DE21 ....44 A1
Briar Lea Cl *DERBYE* DE24 ....52 A5
Briarsgate *DERBYW* DE22 ....33 G1
Briarwood Wy *NORM/LIT* DE23 ....51 F3
Brickkiln La *ILK* DE7 ....20 A3
Brick Rw *DERBYW* DE22 ....34 B2
Brick St *DERBY* DE1 ....33 H5
The Brickyard *ILK* DE7 ....21 G4
Brickyard La *BPR/DUF* DE56 ....13 G1
Bridge Cottages
   BWSH/BRSTN * DE72 ....47 G3
Bridge Fld *BWSH/BRSTN* DE72 ......57 F2
Bridge Foot *BPR/DUF* DE56.............5 H2
Bridge Hl *BPR/DUF* DE56 ....5 H2
Bridgeness Rd *NORM/LIT* DE23 ......50 C3
Bridgeport Rd *DERBYE* DE21 ....36 B5
Bridge St *DERBY* DE1......................2 A2
Bridge Vw *BPR/DUF* DE56 ....12 B3
Bridgwater Cl *DERBYSE* DE24 ....54 B2
Bridle Cl *MELB/CHEL* DE73 ....63 H3
Brierfield Wy *MCKLVR* DE3 ....50 B1
Brigden Av *DERBYSE* DE24 ....53 G1
Brighton Rd *DERBYSE* DE24 ....53 G1
Brightstone Cl *DERBYSE* DE24 ....54 B3
Bright St *DERBY* DE22 ....41 F1
Brigmore Wk *DERBYE* * DE21 ....35 E2
Brindley Cl *DERBYSE* * DE24 ....53 F3
Brisbane Rd *MCKLVR* DE3 ....40 B2
Briset Cl *DERBYSE* DE24 ....61 G2
Bristol Dr *MCKLVR* DE3 ....40 B4
Broad Bank *DERBYW* DE22.............33 H3
Broadfields *DERBYW* DE22 ....34 A3
Broad La *BWSH/BRSTN* DE72 ....55 F5
Broadleaf Cl *DERBYE* DE21 ....35 F1
Broadstone Cl *DERBYE* DE21 ....35 H2
Broadstone La
   MELB/CHEL DE73.................74 D5
Broadway *BPR/DUF* DE56 ....17 G5
   DERBYW DE22.....................33 H3
Broadway Park Cl
   DERBYW DE22.....................33 H3
Brockley *DERBYE* DE21 ....44 D1
Bromley St *DERBYW* DE22 ....33 H4
Brompton Rd *DERBYW* DE22 ....32 C5
Bronte Pl *NORM/LIT* DE23 ....51 E1
Brook Cl *DERBYE* DE21 ....25 F4
   RDERBYSW DE65..................60 A3
Brookdale Dr *NORM/LIT* DE23.........50 A5
Brookfield *MELB/CHEL* DE73 ....68 B1
Brookfield Av *DERBYE* DE21 ....36 A3
   NORM/LIT DE23...................51 G3

Brookfields *BPR/DUF* DE56 ....13 H
Brookfields Dr *ILK* DE7 ....27 E
Brookhouse St *DERBYSE* DE24 ......54 A
Brooklands Dr *NORM/LIT* DE23 ....51 F
Brook Rd *BWSH/BRSTN* DE72 ....45 C
   BWSH/BRSTN DE72................55 F
Brook Side *BPR/DUF* DE56 ....6 A
Brookside Cl *DERBYW* DE22 ....33 F
Brookside Rd *ILK* DE7 ....27 F
Brook St *DERBY* DE1 ....2 A
   HEANOR DE75 ....9 C
Brookvale Av *RIPLEY* DE5 ....7 H
Brookvale Ri *RIPLEY* DE5 ....7 H
Brookvale Rd *RIPLEY* DE5 ....7 H
Broom Cl *BPR/DUF* DE56 ....5 H
   BPR/DUF DE56 ....17 C
   DERBYSE DE24 ....61 C
   MELB/CHEL DE73.................63 C
Broomhill Cl *MCKLVR* DE3 ....40 A
Brough St *DERBYW* DE22 ....41 C
Broughton Av *NORM/LIT* DE23 ....41 C
Browning St *NORM/LIT* DE23 ....52 A
Brown's La *BPR/DUF* DE56 ....13 H
Brun La *ASHB* DE6 ....31 C
Brunswick St *NORM/LIT* DE23 ....42 A
Brunswood Cl *DERBYE* DE21 ....44 D
Brunton Cl *MCKLVR* DE3 ....39 H
Bryony Cl *DERBYE* DE21 ....35 H
Buchanan St *DERBY* DE1 ....2 C
Buchan St *DERBYSE* DE24 ....53 E
Buckford La *RDERBYSW* DE65 ....60 B
Buckhazels La *ASHB* DE6 ....23 F
Buckingham Av *DERBYE* DE21 ....35 E
Buckland Cl *DERBYW* DE22 ....33 H
Buckminster Cl *DERBYE* DE21.........35 C
Buller St *NORM/LIT* DE23 ....41 H
Bullpit La *BPR/DUF* DE56 ....18 B
Bunting Cl *MCKLVR* DE3 ....40 C
Burbage Cl *BPR/DUF* DE56...............7 E
Burbage Pl *DERBYSE* DE24 ....54 C
Burdock Cl *DERBYE* DE21 ....35 F
Burghley Cl *MELB/CHEL* DE73 ....63 C
Burghley Wy *NORM/LIT* DE23 ....50 B
Burleigh Dr *DERBYW* DE22 ....34 A
Burley Dr *DERBYW* DE22 ....25 H
Burley Hl *DERBYW* DE22 ....26 B
Burley La *DERBYW* DE22 ....25 C
Burlington Cl
   BWSH/BRSTN DE72................57 C
Burlington Rd *DERBYSE* DE24 ....32 C
Burlington Wy *MCKLVR* DE3 ....40 A
The Burma Rd *ASHB* DE6 ....22 A
Burnaby St *DERBYSE* DE24 ....53 C
Burnham Dr *MCKLVR* DE3 ....39 H
Burns Cl *NORM/LIT* DE23 ....51 E
Burnside Cl *DERBYSE* DE24 ....61 C
Burnside Dr *DERBYE* DE21 ....45 E
Burnside St *DERBYSE* DE24 ....53 H
Burrows Wk *DERBY* DE1...................2 C
Burton Rd *DERBY* DE1 ....2 C
   NORM/LIT DE23...................41 F
   RDERBYSW DE65..................59 E
Bute Wk *DERBY* * DE22 ....34 D
Buttermere Dr *DERBYW* DE22 ....25 H
Butterwick Cl *NORM/LIT* DE23 ....51 H
Buttonoak Dr *MELB/CHEL* DE73 ......63 H
The Butts *BPR/DUF* DE56.................6 B
Buxton Dr *DERBYE* DE21 ....18 D
   MCKLVR DE3 ....40 B
Buxton Houses *DERBYE* * DE21 .....44 D
Buxton Rd *DERBYE* DE21 ....35 C
Byfield Cl *DERBYE* DE21 ....36 A
Byng Av *NORM/LIT* DE23 ....52 A
Byron St *NORM/LIT* DE23 ....42 A
Bywell La *BPR/DUF* DE56 ....13 C

C

Cadgwith Dr *DERBYW* DE22............33 F
Cadwell Cl *DERBYSE* DE24 ....54 C
Caerhays Ct *DERBYSE* DE24 ....61 C
Caernarvon Cl *DERBYE* DE21 ....45 E
Caesar St *DERBY* DE1 ....34 C
Cairngorm Dr *DERBYSE* DE24 ....61 C
Cairns Cl *MCKLVR* DE3 ....40 B
Calder Cl *DERBYW* DE22 ....25 H
Caldermill Dr *DERBYE* DE21 ....35 H
California Gdns *DERBYW* DE22 ....41 F
Calke Rd *MELB/CHEL* * DE73 ....75 H
Calladine La *ILK* DE7 ....14 C
Callow Hill Wy *NORM/LIT* DE23 ......50 C
Calver Cl *BPR/DUF* DE56 ....6 C
   DERBYE DE21 ....27 F
Calverton Cl *DERBYSE* DE24...........63 F
Calvert St *DERBY* DE1 ....3 G
Calvin Cl *DERBYSE* DE24 ....53 H

amberwell Av *DERBYW* DE22 ......**32** D5
amborne Cl *DERBYE* DE21 ......**35** F2
ambridge St *DERBYE* DE21 ......**44** D3
NORM/LIT DE23......................**42** B4
amden St *DERBYE* DE21 ......**41** G2
amellia Cl *MCKLVR* DE3............**40** A3
ameron Rd *NORM/LIT* DE23......**52** A1
ampbell St *BPR/DUF* DE56..........**6** A4
DERBYSE DE24........................**53** E3
ampion Hl *CDON/KEG* DE74......**72** D3
ampion St *DERBYE* DE21 ......**41** G1
ampsie Ct *DERBYSE* DE24..........**61** G1
amp St *DERBY* DE1 ......**34** B4
anada St *BPR/DUF* DE56..............**6** B5
anal Bank *BWSH/BRSTN* DE72....**66** D3
anal St *MELB/CHEL* * DE73..........**3** F7
anal St *DERBY* DE1 ....**3** F7
anderson Rd *MCKLVR* DE3 ......**40** B4
anon's Wk *DERBYW* DE22 ......**34** A1
anterbury Cl *BPR/DUF* * DE56.....**17** H1
anterbury St *DERBYE* DE21 ......**35** F2
antley Cl *MCKLVR* DE3 ......**40** A3
ardales Cl *RDERBYSW* * DE65......**60** A2
ardean Cl *DERBYE* DE21 ......**34** C4
ardigan St *DERBYE* DE21 ......**35** E4
ardinal Cl *DERBYE* DE21 ......**35** G1
ardrona Cl *DERBYE* DE21 ......**35** G1
arisbrooke Gdns
 NORM/LIT DE23......................**51** F3
arlin Cl *BWSH/BRSTN* DE72......**57** H1
arlisle Av *NORM/LIT* DE21 ......**51** E1
arlton Av *DERBYSE* DE24 ......**53** F5
arlton St *DERBYSE* DE24 ......**53** F5
arlton Gdns *DERBYSE* DE24 ......**53** F5
arlton Rd *NORM/LIT* DE23 ......**41** C5
arlyle St *DERBYSE* DE24 ......**52** A4
arnegie St *NORM/LIT* DE24 ......**52** A1
arnforth Cl *MCKLVR* DE3..........**40** B5
arnival Wy *CDON/KEG* DE74......**73** F3
arnoustie Cl *MCKLVR* DE3 ......**40** C4
arol Crs *DERBYE* DE21............**43** G2
aroline Cl *DERBYSE* DE24 ......**54** B2
arr Flds *ILK* DE7 ....**14** B3
arriers Rd *RDERBYSW* DE65......**58** B5
arrington St *DERBY* DE1............**3** F6
arron Cl *DERBYSE* DE24 ......**51** H5
arrs Cl *CDON/KEG* DE74............**72** D4
arsington Crs *DERBYW* DE22 ......**33** G2
arsington Ms *DERBYW* DE22 ......**33** G2
arson Rd *DERBYE* DE21 ......**36** A5
arter St *DERBYSE* DE24 ......**53** E3
ascade Gv *NORM/LIT* DE23......**50** D2
asson St *DERBYSE* DE24 ......**53** H3
astings Rd *NORM/LIT* DE23 ......**52** C1
astle Cl *BWSH/BRSTN* DE72......**46** A4
astlecraig Ct *DERBYSE* DE24......**61** G1
astle Cft *DERBYSE* DE24 ......**54** C4
astle Hl *BPR/DUF* DE56............**17** H1
CDON/KEG DE74......................**73** E3
RDERBYSW DE65......................**60** A3
astle La *MELB/CHEL* DE73 ......**76** A3
astle Ms *MELB/CHEL* DE73 ......**76** A3
astle Mills *MELB/CHEL* DE73 ......**76** A3
astle Orch *BPR/DUF* DE56 ......**17** H1
astleshaw Dr *NORM/LIT* DE23 ......**50** B2
astle St *DERBY* DE1 ....**2** E5
astleton Av *NORM/LIT* DE23 ......**52** A1
athedral Rd *DERBY* DE1 ......**2** B2
athedral Vw *DERBY* DE1......**2** B2
atherine St *NORM/LIT* DE23......**42** C4
atterick Dr *MCKLVR* DE3............**39** H5
auseway *DERBYW* DE22 ......**33** H1
avan Dr *DERBY* DE1 ......**44** A2
avendish Av *DERBYW* DE22 ......**26** A5
avendish Cl *BPR/DUF* DE56 ......**17** G3
BWSH/BRSTN DE72....................**66** D2
CDON/KEG DE74......................**72** D5
avendish Ct
 BWSH/BRSTN DE72....................**66** D3
DERBY DE1 ....**2** B3
avendish St *DERBY* DE1 ......**2** B3
avendish Wy *MCKLVR* DE3 ......**40** B4
aversfield Cl *NORM/LIT* DE23......**50** D1
axton Cl *NORM/LIT* DE23............**52** C1
axton St *NORM/LIT* DE23 ......**51** H2
ecil St *DERBYW* DE22..................**41** C1
edar Cft *BPR/DUF* DE56............**14** A3
BWSH/BRSTN DE72....................**65** F5
edar Dr *BWSH/BRSTN* DE72......**45** H2
edar Gv *BPR/DUF* DE56 ......**6** D2
edar Rd *CDON/KEG* DE74............**73** E5
edar St *DERBYW* DE22 ......**33** H4
edarwood Ct *DERBYE* DE21......**35** G1
elandine Cl *DERBYE* DE21......**35** G1
elanese Rd *DERBYE* DE21......**44** B3
emetery Hill Nottingham Rd
 DERBYE DE21 ....**3** K2
emetery Rd *BPR/DUF* DE56..........**6** B1

Centenary Wy *ASHB* DE6 ......**16** A3
BPR/DUF DE56 ......**18** C3
Central Av *BWSH/BRSTN* DE72 ......**45** C5
ILK DE7......................**21** C3
Centre Ct *DERBY* DE1............**42** C3
Chaddesden La *DERBYE* DE21......**43** C1
Chaddesden Park Rd
 DERBYE DE21......................**35** G5
Chadfield Rd *BPR/DUF* DE56......**11** H5
Chadwick Av *DERBYSE* DE24......**53** F4
Chaffinch Cl *DERBYSE* DE21......**37** E5
Chain La *MCKLVR* DE3 ......**40** D4
Chalfont Sq *DERBYE* DE21 ......**36** A1
Chalkley Cl *DERBYSE* DE24 ......**53** C2
Challis Av *DERBYSE* DE24 ......**36** A4
Chambers St *DERBYE* DE21 ......**53** F1
Champion Hl *BPR/DUF* DE56......**17** H1
Chancel Pl *DERBYW* * DE22 ......**2** B7
Chandlers Ford *DERBYE* DE21......**35** G1
Chandos Pole St *DERBYW* DE22 ......**33** C5
Chandres Ct *DERBYW* DE22 ......**25** H4
Chandwick Ct *DERBYSE* DE24......**61** C1
Chantry Cl *MCKLVR* DE3............**39** H5
Chapel La *DERBYE* DE21 ......**35** H4
DERBYE DE21......................**44** D1
MELB/CHEL DE73......................**63** H3
MELB/CHEL DE73......................**68** B1
Chapel Rw *BWSH/BRSTN* DE72 ......**45** C4
Chapel Side *DERBYE* * DE21 ......**44** D1
Chapel St *BPR/DUF* DE56 ......**6** A4
BPR/DUF DE56......................**12** D3
BPR/DUF DE56......................**13** F2
BPR/DUF DE56......................**17** H2
DERBY DE1......................**2** B2
DERBYE DE21......................**44** D1
MELB/CHEL DE73......................**74** D1
MELB/CHEL DE73......................**76** A3
Chapman Av *DERBYSE* DE24 ......**54** A3
Chapter Cl *DERBYE* DE21 ......**35** E1
Charing Ct *DERBY* DE1............**34** C4
Charingworth Rd *DERBYW* DE22 ......**36** A1
Chariot Cl *DERBYSE* DE24 ......**54** C4
Charlbury Cl *NORM/LIT* DE23......**50** D1
Charles Av *DERBYE* DE21 ......**36** C5
Charleston Rd *DERBYE* DE21......**36** B5
Charlestown Dr *DERBYW* DE22......**25** C4
Charlotte St *NORM/LIT* DE23 ......**42** B4
Charnwood Av *BPR/DUF* DE56 ......**6** A3
BWSH/BRSTN DE72....................**45** H4
CDON/KEG DE74......................**73** F4
NORM/LIT DE23......................**51** C4
Charnwood St *DERBY* DE1 ......**2** C7
Charterhouse Cl *DERBYE* DE21......**27** F5
Charterstone La *DERBYW* DE22 ......**25** H4
Chartwell Dr *DERBYE* DE21......**3** H3
The Chase *BPR/DUF* DE56 ......**14** A2
DERBYE DE21......................**19** E3
DERBYSE DE24......................**52** A5
Chase Cl *MELB/CHEL* DE73......**64** A2
Chatham Ct *BPR/DUF* DE56 ......**7** E3
Chatham St *NORM/LIT* DE23 ......**52** B1
Chatsworth Crs *DERBYW* DE22 ......**34** A1
Chatsworth Dr *DERBYE* DE21 ......**19** E3
MCKLVR DE3......................**40** B3
Chatsworth St *NORM/LIT* DE23......**41** H5
Chatteris Dr *DERBYE* DE21 ......**35** E2
Cheadle Cl *MCKLVR* DE3............**41** E5
Cheam Cl *DERBYW* DE22............**32** B5
Cheapside *BPR/DUF* DE56 ......**6** A4
DERBY DE1......................**2** B3
Chedworth Dr *DERBYSE* DE24......**54** C3
Chellaston La *MELB/CHEL* DE73 ......**64** B3
Chellaston Park Ct
 MELB/CHEL DE73......................**63** G3
Chellaston Rd *DERBYSE* DE24......**53** F4
Chelmarsh Cl *MELB/CHEL* DE73......**63** H1
Chelmorton Pl *DERBYE* DE21 ......**35** G3
Chelmsford Cl *MCKLVR* DE3......**39** H3
Chelsea Cl *DERBYW* DE22 ......**32** B5
Chelwood Rd *MELB/CHEL* DE73 ......**63** G2
Chequers La *DERBYE* DE21 ......**3** J3
Chequers Rd *DERBYE* DE21......**3** J3
Cheribough Rd *CDON/KEG* DE74......**72** D5
Cheriton Gdns *NORM/LIT* DE23 ......**50** B2
Cherry Cl *BWSH/BRSTN* DE72......**57** H1
Cherrybrook Dr *DERBYE* DE21 ......**28** A5
Cherrydale Ct *NORM/LIT* DE23 ......**50** D3
Cherry Tree Av *BPR/DUF* DE56 ......**6** B1
Cherry Tree Ms *DERBYE* DE21 ......**44** A2
Chertsey Rd *MCKLVR* DE3............**39** H4
Chesapeake Rd *DERBYE* DE21......**36** A5
Cheshire St *DERBYSE* DE24 ......**53** E4
Chester Av *DERBYW* DE22 ......**26** C3
Chesterfield Houses
 DERBY * DE21 ....**44** D3
Chesterfield Rd *BPR/DUF* DE56......**6** B3
Chesterford Ct *NORM/LIT* DE23......**50** C3
Chester Green Rd *DERBY* DE1......**34** B4

Chester Pk *DERBYE* * DE21 ......**34** C3
Chesterton Av *NORM/LIT* DE23......**51** H2
Chesterton Rd *DERBYE* DE21......**36** D5
Chestnut Av *BPR/DUF* DE56 ......**6** B5
BPR/DUF DE56......................**12** D3
MCKLVR DE3......................**40** B3
MELB/CHEL DE73......................**63** G1
NORM/LIT DE23......................**42** B4
Chestnut Cl *BPR/DUF* DE56 ......**17** H3
ILK DE7......................**14** B3
Chestnut Gv *BWSH/BRSTN* DE72....**45** H5
RDERBYSW DE65......................**48** A5
Chevely Ct *DERBYSE* DE24 ......**35** E3
Cheverton Cl *DERBYSE* DE24 ......**54** C4
Chevin Av *BWSH/BRSTN* DE72 ......**45** H4
MCKLVR DE3......................**40** C4
Chevin Bank *BPR/DUF* DE56......**11** H5
Chevin Rd *BPR/DUF* DE56 ......**5** C3
BPR/DUF DE56......................**11** H5
DERBYW DE22......................**34** A4
Chevin Side *BPR/DUF* * DE56......**12** A1
Chevin V *BPR/DUF* DE56............**11** H5
Chevin Vw *BPR/DUF* * DE56..........**6** A4
Cheviot St *DERBYW* DE22 ......**41** F1
Cheyenne Gdns *DERBYE* DE21......**44** A1
Chilson Dr *MCKLVR* DE3 ......**39** H3
Chime Cl *DERBYE* DE21............**35** H2
Chingford Ct *DERBYW* DE22 ......**41** E1
Chinley Rd *DERBYE* DE21 ......**35** H2
Chiswick Cl *DERBYW* DE22 ......**32** C5
Church Cl *MELB/CHEL* DE73 ......**63** H3
MELB/CHEL * DE73......................**69** E4
Church Ct *RIPLEY* * DE5............**14** C1
Churchdown Cl *DERBYE* DE21......**36** A4
Church Hl *RDERBYSW* DE65......**48** A4
Churchill Cl *BWSH/BRSTN* DE72....**57** C1
Church La *ASHB* DE6............**30** D1
BPR/DUF DE56......................**73** E4
CDON/KEG DE74......................**73** C3
DERBYE DE21......................**26** D1
DERBYE DE21......................**31** H5
DERBYW DE22......................**32** C3
DERBYW DE22......................**34** B1
ILK DE7......................**14** C4
ILK DE7......................**27** F4
ILK DE7......................**28** D2
MELB/CHEL DE73......................**68** B2
Church La North *DERBYW* DE22 ......**26** A5
Church Ms *DERBYE* DE21 ......**44** C2
Church Rd *DERBYW* DE22 ......**25** F2
Churchside Wk *DERBYW* * DE22 ......**2** A6
Church Sq *MELB/CHEL* DE73 ......**76** A4
Church St *BPR/DUF* DE56 ......**12** D4
BPR/DUF DE56......................**45** H2
BWSH/BRSTN DE72....................**45** H2
DERBYE DE21......................**13** G5
DERBYE DE21......................**44** C2
DERBYSE DE24......................**54** B1
MELB/CHEL DE73......................**76** A3
NORM/LIT DE23......................**41** F5
RIPLEY DE5......................**42** B4
Church Vw *BWSH/BRSTN* DE72 ......**57** H2
HEANOR DE75......................**9** G3
Church Wk *BPR/DUF* DE56 ......**6** A4
City Rd *DERBY* DE1 ......**34** B4
Clapgun St *CDON/KEG* DE74......**73** E4
Clarence Rd *NORM/LIT* DE23 ......**41** H5
Clarke Av *HEANOR* DE75............**9** H5
Clarkes La *BWSH/BRSTN* DE72 ......**65** C4
Clarke St *DERBY* DE1............**3** F1
Clay St *BWSH/BRSTN* DE72......**56** D2
Clayton Gv *HEANOR* DE75............**9** H3
Clement Rd *ILK* DE7............**14** B3
Cleveland Av
 BWSH/BRSTN DE72....................**56** C2
DERBYE DE21......................**44** A1
Clifford St *DERBYSE* DE24 ......**43** E4
Clifton Dr *MCKLVR* DE3............**40** B3
Clifton Rd *DERBYW* DE22 ......**25** C5
Clifton St *DERBY* DE1............**2** A5
Clinton St *DERBYE* DE21 ......**3** K2
Clipstone Gdns *DERBYE* DE21......**44** A1
Cloisters Ct *DERBYE* DE21......**27** G5
The Close *DERBYW* DE22 ......**34** A1
NORM/LIT DE23......................**41** G4
Cloudwood Cl *NORM/LIT* DE23 ......**45** E1
Clover Cl *DERBYE* DE21............**35** H1
Clover Ct *BWSH/BRSTN* DE72......**66** B2
Cloverdale Dr *DERBYE* DE21 ......**44** A2
Cloverslade *RDERBYSW* DE65 ......**59** H3
Cloves Hl *ILK* DE7............**20** B3
Club La *MELB/CHEL* DE73 ......**68** B2
Cluster Ct *BPR/DUF* * DE56 ......**6** A3
Cluster Rd *BPR/DUF* DE56 ......**6** A3

Clusters Ct *BPR/DUF* DE56..........**6** A3
Coach Dr *DERBYW* DE22............**25** F1
Cobden St *DERBYE* DE21 ......**41** C1
Cobham Cl *DERBYE* DE24 ......**61** C1
Cobthorn Dr *DERBYE* DE22......**25** F4
Coburn Pl *DERBY* * DE1............**2** B4
Cockayne St North
 DERBYSE DE24......................**53** F3
Cockayne St South
 DERBYSE DE24......................**53** F3
Cockshut La *MELB/CHEL* DE73 ......**75** C3
Cod Beck Cl *DERBYSE* DE24......**54** B3
Codnor-Denby La *RIPLEY* DE5 ......**9** F2
Coke St *DERBYW* DE22............**41** G2
Cole La *BWSH/BRSTN* DE72......**45** H2
Coleman St *DERBYSE* DE24 ......**53** F2
Coleraine Cl *DERBYE* DE21 ......**44** A2
Coleridge St *NORM/LIT* DE23 ......**52** A3
College Ms *DERBY* DE1............**41** H1
Collier La *BWSH/BRSTN* DE72......**45** H2
Collingham Gdns *DERBYW* DE22......**40** D1
Collis Cl *DERBYSE* DE24 ......**53** F2
Collumbell Av
 BWSH/BRSTN DE72....................**45** H1
Colombo St *NORM/LIT* DE23 ......**42** C5
Coltsfoot Dr *DERBYSE* DE24........**62** A2
Columbine Cl *DERBYE* DE21 ......**35** H2
Colville St *DERBYW* DE22 ......**33** C5
Colwell Dr *DERBYSE* DE24 ......**54** C4
Colwyn Av *NORM/LIT* DE23 ......**41** C5
Colyear St *DERBY* DE1............**2** C4
Comfrey Cl *NORM/LIT* DE23 ......**50** C3
Commerce St *DERBYSE* DE24 ......**53** C1
MELB/CHEL DE73......................**75** H3
The Common *DERBYW* DE22 ......**17** F5
Common La *ILK* DE7............**29** F1
Common Piece La
 RDERBYSW DE65......................**60** B3
Compton Av *BWSH/BRSTN* DE72....**65** F4
Compton Cl *DERBYSE* DE24 ......**54** B3
Coniston Av *DERBYE* DE21 ......**36** D5
Coniston Crs *DERBYE* DE21 ......**35** E1
Connaught Rd *DERBYW* DE22 ......**41** F2
Consett Cl *DERBYE* DE21 ......**35** E2
Consort Gdns *DERBYE* DE21 ......**28** B5
Constable Av *DERBYW* DE22 ......**41** F1
Constable Dr *NORM/LIT* DE23 ......**41** F1
Constable La *NORM/LIT* DE23......**41** F4
Conway Av *BWSH/BRSTN* DE72 ......**46** A4
Cook Cl *BPR/DUF* DE56............**7** F2
Cookham Cl *MCKLVR* DE3............**39** H4
Cooks Av *CDON/KEG* DE74 ......**72** D4
Co-operative St *NORM/LIT* DE23 ......**42** A4
Coopers Cl *BWSH/BRSTN* DE72 ......**46** A5
Cooper St *DERBYSE* DE24 ......**33** F5
Copeland St *DERBY* DE1 ......**2** E5
Copes Wy *DERBYE* DE21 ......**35** H3
Copperleaf Cl *DERBYW* DE22 ......**2** A6
Copper Yd *RIPLEY* DE5............**9** E5
The Coppice *BPR/DUF* * DE56......**6** B4
Coppice Cl *BPR/DUF* DE56......**13** H2
DERBYW DE22......................**34** A2
Coppicewood Dr
 NORM/LIT DE23......................**40** D5
Copse Gv *NORM/LIT* DE23..........**50** D2
Corbel Cl *DERBYE* DE21 ......**35** F1
Corbridge Gv *NORM/LIT* DE23......**50** D2
Corby Cl *DERBYE* DE24 ......**53** C4
Corden Av *MCKLVR* DE3............**40** D4
Corden St *NORM/LIT* DE23 ......**42** B4
Cordville Cl *DERBYE* DE21......**44** A1
Cordwell Cl *CDON/KEG* DE74......**72** C4
Corfe Cl *NORM/LIT* DE23............**51** C3
Coriander Gdns *NORM/LIT* DE23......**51** C5
Corinium Cl *DERBYSE* DE24......**54** C4
Cornflower Dr *DERBYE* DE21 ......**35** H1
Cornhill *DERBYW* DE22............**26** A4
Corn Market *DERBY* DE1............**2** D3
Cornmill Cl *DERBYSE* DE24 ......**54** C4
Cornwall Rd *DERBYE* DE21......**3** K1
Coronation Av *BPR/DUF* DE56 ......**6** B2
DERBYSE DE24......................**53** F2
Coronation Cl *MELB/CHEL* DE73 ......**75** H2
Coronation Cottages
 BWSH/BRSTN DE72....................**57** F4
Coronation Rd *ILK* DE7............**29** C2
Coronation St *NORM/LIT* DE23......**52** C1
Coronet Ct *DERBYE* DE21 ......**28** C5
Corporation St *DERBY* DE1 ......**2** D3
Cotswold Cl *DERBYE* DE21......**51** F1
Cottisford Cl *NORM/LIT* DE23......**50** D1
Cotton Brook Rd
 NORM/LIT DE23......................**52** C1
Cotton La *DERBYSE* DE24 ......**52** C1
Countisbury Dr *DERBYE* DE21......**35** H1
The Court *DERBYSE* DE24 ......**54** A3
Courtland Dr *DERBYSE* DE24 ......**53** H3
Courtland Gdns *DERBYSE* DE24......**54** A3

Courtland Rd *RDERBYSW* DE65 ....**58** B1
Courtney Wy *BPR/DUF* DE56 ....**7** E2
The Covert *DERBYE* DE21 ....**44** D2
Cowdray Cl *DERBYSE* DE24 ....**61** G2
Cowley St *DERBYW* DE22 ....**33** H4
Cowlishaw Cl
  BWSH/BRSTN DE72.............**66** B3
Cowper St *DERBYSE* DE24 ....**52** B4
Cowsley Rd *DERBYE* DE21 ....**35** E4
Coxbench Rd *DERBYE* DE21 ....**19** F1
Cox Green Ct *NORM/LIT* DE23 .....**50** C2
Coxon St *DERBYE* DE21..................**44** D1
Crabtree Cl *CDON/KEG* DE74 ....**72** D5
  DERBYW DE22..............................**25** F4
Crab Tree Hl *DERBYE* DE21 ....**18** D5
Crabtree Hill Keddleston Rd
  DERBYW DE22..............................**25** F5
Craddock Av *DERBYE* DE21 ....**44** D3
Craiglee Ct *DERBYSE* DE24 ....**61** G1
Cranberry Gv *NORM/LIT* DE23 .....**50** C3
Cranhill Cl *NORM/LIT* DE23 ....**50** C3
Cranmer Rd *DERBYE* DE21 ....**3** G3
Crawley Rd *DERBYE* DE21 ....**53** G4
Crayford Rd *DERBYSE* DE24..........**53** H4
Crecy Cl *NORM/LIT* DE23...............**41** F3
The Crescent
  BWSH/BRSTN DE72.............**57** F2
  DERBYE DE21 ....**43** G1
  DERBYSE DE24 ....**53** F4
  ILK DE7 ....**14** B3
  ILK DE7 ....**21** G4
Cressbrook Wy *DERBYE* DE21 .....**28** A5
The Crest *DERBYW* DE22..............**33** H1
Cresta Gv *DERBYE* DE21 ....**35** C2
Crewe St *NORM/LIT* DE23 ....**42** A5
Crewton Wy *DERBYSE* DE24 ....**53** C2
Crich Av *NORM/LIT* DE23 ....**41** E4
Crich La *BPR/DUF* DE56.................**6** B1
Cricklewood Rd *DERBYW* DE22....**33** E5
Cringle Ms *DERBYE* DE21 ....**35** F1
The Croft *BPR/DUF* DE56 ....**12** D1
  BWSH/BRSTN DE72.............**56** D3
  ILK DE7 ....**20** B4
  MELB/CHEL DE73.......................**75** H2
  NORM/LIT DE23...........................**51** C1
Croft Cl *BWSH/BRSTN* DE72 ....**45** H1
  DERBYE DE21 ....**37** E5
Croft End *DERBYE* DE21 ....**18** D5
Crofters Ct *DERBYE* DE21 ....**35** F1
Croft La *DERBYE* DE21 ....**27** E5
Cromarty Cl *DERBYSE* DE24 ....**51** H5
Cromer Cl *MCKLVR* DE3 ....**39** H5
Cromford Dr *MCKLVR* DE3 ....**40** A2
Cromford Rd *DERBYE* DE21 ....**35** H3
Crompton St *DERBY* DE1 ....**2** B5
Cromwell Av *RDERBYSW* DE65......**60** A2
Cromwell Rd *NORM/LIT* DE23 ......**42** A4
Cropton Cl *DERBYSE* DE24 ....**54** B3
Crosby St *DERBYW* DE22 ....**41** G3
Cross Cl *NORM/LIT* DE23 ....**51** F1
Crossdale Gv *DERBYE* DE21 ....**28** B5
Crosshill *RIPLEY* DE5 ....**9** G1
Cross St *DERBYW* DE22 ....**33** G5
Crown Hill Wy *ILK* DE7 ....**21** G5
Crownland Dr *MELB/CHEL* DE73....**63** H2
Crown Ms *DERBYW* DE22..............**41** H3
Crown St *BPR/DUF* DE56 ....**17** H1
  DERBYW DE22..............................**41** H3
Crown Ter *DERBY* DE1 ....**2** D4
Crown Wk *DERBY* DE1 ....**2** D4
Crown Wy *MELB/CHEL* DE73 ....**63** G4
Crowshaw St *DERBYSE* DE24........**52** C1
Cuckmere Cl *DERBYW* DE22 ....**26** C3
Culworth Cl *BPR/DUF* DE56 ....**7** E3
Cumberhills Rd *DERBYW* DE22 .....**17** E4
Cumberland Av *DERBYE* DE21.......**35** F5
Cumberland Crs
  BWSH/BRSTN DE72.............**45** C5
Cumbria Wk *MCKLVR* DE3.............**39** H5
Cummings St *NORM/LIT* DE23 .....**42** B4
The Cunnery *ASHB* DE6..................**31** E1
Curborough Dr *DERBYSE* DE24 ....**54** B3
Curlew Cl *NORM/LIT* DE23............**51** C5
Curzon Cl *DERBYW* DE22 ....**25** F4
Curzon Ct *BPR/DUF* DE56 ....**18** A2
  MCKLVR DE3 ....**40** A5
Curzon La *BPR/DUF* DE56.............**17** G2
  DERBYSE DE24 ....**53** H1
Curzon Rd *DERBYE* DE21 ....**35** G2
Curzon St *DERBY* DE1 ....**2** B4
Cuttlebrook Cl *NORM/LIT* DE23 ...**51** H4

D

Dahlia Dr *DERBYE* DE21 ....**28** B5
Dairy House Rd *NORM/LIT* DE23 ..**42** B5

Dale Cl *BWSH/BRSTN* DE72 ....**57** G1
Dale Ct *BPR/DUF* DE56 ....**13** G2
Dale Park Av *BPR/DUF* DE56 ....**13** H2
Dale Rd *DERBYE* DE21 ....**37** F5
  DERBYE DE24 ....**54** B2
  ILK DE7 ....**29** H4
  NORM/LIT DE23...........................**42** A4
Dalesgate Cl *NORM/LIT* DE23.......**51** E4
Dale View Gdns *BPR/DUF* DE56 ...**13** G2
Dalkeith Av *DERBYSE* DE24 ....**53** G4
Dalley La *BPR/DUF* DE56 ....**5** F1
Dalness Ct *DERBYSE* DE24 ....**61** G1
Dalton Av *DERBYW* DE22 ....**41** F3
Danebridge Crs *DERBYE* DE21 .....**35** H2
Danesby Crs *RIPLEY* DE5 ....**13** G1
Danesby Ri *RIPLEY* DE5 ....**13** H1
Darby St *NORM/LIT* DE23..............**42** A4
Dark La *BPR/DUF* DE56 ....**12** B4
Darley Abbey Dr *DERBYW* DE22 ..**34** A2
Darley Gv *DERBYW* DE22 ....**34** B2
Darley La *DERBY* DE1 ....**2** C1
Darley Park Dr *DERBYW* DE22......**34** A2
Darley Park Rd *DERBYW* DE22 .....**34** A2
Darley St *DERBYW* DE22 ....**34** B2
Darsway *CDON/KEG* DE74.............**72** D5
Dartford Pl *DERBYSE* DE24 ....**53** H4
Darwin Av *DERBYSE* DE24 ....**53** E5
Darwin Rd *MCKLVR* DE3................**40** B3
Dashwood St *NORM/LIT* DE23......**42** B3
Datchet Cl *DERBYSE* DE24 ....**50** D1
Davenport Rd *DERBYSE* DE24 ......**52** D1
Daventry Cl *MCKLVR* DE3 ....**39** H3
David's Cl *MELB/CHEL* DE73 ....**63** F3
Dawlish Ct *DERBYSE* DE24 ....**54** B2
Dawsmere Cl *DERBYE* DE21 ....**35** E2
Daylesford Cl *NORM/LIT* DE23 .....**50** D1
Days La *BPR/DUF* DE56 ....**6** A4
Dayton Cl *DERBYE* DE21 ....**44** B1
Deacon Cl *DERBYE* DE21 ....**35** F1
Deadman's La *DERBYSE* DE24 ......**43** E4
Dean Cl *NORM/LIT* DE23 ....**50** D4
Deans Dr *BWSH/BRSTN* DE72.......**45** G4
Dean St *DERBYW* DE22 ....**41** H3
Deborah Dr *DERBYE* DE21 ....**35** H4
Dee Cl *DERBYSE* DE24 ....**61** H1
Dee La *RDERBYSW* DE65 ....**49** E2
Deep Dale La *DERBYSE* DE24 ....**61** H2
Deepdale Rd *BPR/DUF* DE56 ....**6** C3
  DERBYE DE21 ....**45** E3
Deer Park Vw *DERBYE* DE21 ....**37** E5
De Ferrers Cl *BPR/DUF* * DE56 ....**17** H2
Degge St *DERBY* DE1 ....**2** C5
Deincourt Cl *DERBYE* DE21 ....**37** F5
Delamere Cl *BWSH/BRSTN* DE72 ..**57** G1
  DERBYE DE21 ....**35** H2
Delven La *CDON/KEG* DE74...........**72** D4
Denarth Av *DERBYSE* DE24 ....**63** F1
Denbigh St *DERBYE* DE21 ....**35** F4
Denby Common *RIPLEY* DE5 ....**9** G5
Denby La *RIPLEY* DE5 ....**14** A1
Denison Gdns *DERBYE* DE21 ....**36** A5
Dennis Cl *NORM/LIT* DE23.............**50** B2
Denstone Dr *DERBYSE* DE24 ....**53** H5
Dentdale Ct *DERBYSE* * DE24 ......**54** B3
Denver Rd *MCKLVR* DE3 ....**40** A3
Depedale Av
  BWSH/BRSTN DE72.............**45** H4
Depot St *NORM/LIT* DE23 ....**42** B4
Derby La *NORM/LIT* DE23..............**52** A1
Derby Rd *BPR/DUF* DE56 ....**12** A5
  BPR/DUF DE56 ....**18** A4
  BWSH/BRSTN DE72.............**47** E2
  BWSH/BRSTN DE72.............**56** B1
  BWSH/BRSTN DE72.............**65** F1
  DERBYE DE21 ....**13** E5
  DERBYE DE21 ....**28** D5
  DERBYE DE21 ....**44** B2
  MELB/CHEL DE73.......................**63** G2
  MELB/CHEL DE73.......................**75** H2
  RIPLEY DE5 ....**8** D1
Derrington Leys *DERBYSE* DE24 ...**54** C3
Derventio Cl *DERBY* DE1...............**34** B4
Derwent Av *BPR/DUF* DE56 ....**12** A2
  BWSH/BRSTN DE72.............**45** H3
  DERBYW DE22..............................**26** C4
Derwent Cl *DERBYW* DE22 ....**26** B4
Derwent Ct *BPR/DUF* DE56 ....**6** C3
  DERBY * DE1 ....**2** D4
  DERBY * DE1 ....**2** D3
Derwent Dr *DERBYSE* DE24 ....**61** G2
Derwent Ri *DERBYE* DE21 ....**45** E2
Derwent Rd *DERBYE* DE21 ....**44** C3
Derwent St *BPR/DUF* DE56 ....**5** H4
  BWSH/BRSTN DE72.............**56** D2
  DERBY DE1 ....**2** E3
Derwent V *BPR/DUF* DE56 ....**6** A5
Derwent Vw *BPR/DUF* DE56 ....**6** A2
  BPR/DUF * DE56 ....**12** B2

Devas Gdns *DERBYE* DE21 ....**44** C1
Devon Cl *DERBYE* DE21 ....**3** K1
Devonshire Av
  BWSH/BRSTN DE72.............**45** H4
  DERBYW DE22..............................**26** A5
Devonshire Dr *BPR/DUF* DE56.......**17** C3
  MCKLVR DE3 ....**40** B3
Dewchurch Dr *NORM/LIT* DE23....**51** E4
  NORM/LIT DE23...........................**51** D4
Dexter St *NORM/LIT* DE23 ....**42** D4
Diamond Dr *DERBYE* DE21 ....**27** G5
Dickens Sq *NORM/LIT* DE23 ....**52** A2
Dickinson St *DERBYE* DE24 ....**43** E4
Diseworth Cl *MELB/CHEL* DE73 ....**63** D2
Dix Av *ILK* DE7 ....**15** E4
Dobholes La *ILK* DE7 ....**14** A4
Dodburn Ct *DERBYSE* DE24 ....**51** C5
Dog La *MELB/CHEL* DE73 ....**76** D4
Doles La *RDERBYSW* DE65 ....**59** H1
Dolphin Cl *DERBYE* DE21 ....**37** F5
Donald Hawley Wy
  BPR/DUF DE56 ....**18** A2
Donington Cl *NORM/LIT* DE23 ......**51** H4
Donington Dr *NORM/LIT* DE23 .....**51** H4
Donington La
  BWSH/BRSTN DE72.............**67** F4
Donington Pk
  CDON/KEG * DE74......................**71** H5
Dorchester Av *DERBYE* DE21 ....**35** F4
Dorking Rd *DERBYW* DE22 ....**33** E5
Dorrien Av *NORM/LIT* DE23 ....**52** A1
Dorset St *DERBYE* DE21 ....**3** K1
Douglas Av *HEANOR* DE75 ....**9** H4
Douglas St *DERBY* DE1 ....**42** D4
Dove Cl *BPR/DUF* DE56 ....**13** H2
  MCKLVR DE3 ....**40** D3
The Dovecote *DERBYE* DE21 ....**13** C4
Dovecote Dr
  BWSH/BRSTN DE72.............**45** F4
Dovedale Av *DERBYSE* DE24 ....**54** B2
Dovedale Cl *RIPLEY* DE5 ....**8** C1
Dovedale Ct *BPR/DUF* * DE56 ......**6** C3
Dovedale Crs *BPR/DUF* DE56........**6** C2
Dovedale Ri *DERBYW* DE22 ....**33** G2
Dovedale Rd *DERBYE* DE21 ....**44** D3
The Dovedales *MCKLVR* * DE3 .....**40** A4
Dover Ct *NORM/LIT* * DE23 ....**42** B4
Dover St *NORM/LIT* DE23 ....**42** B5
Dower Cl *DERBYW* DE22 ....**34** B1
Downham Cl *MCKLVR* DE3 ....**40** B5
Downing Cl *DERBYW* DE22 ....**32** C5
Downing Rd *DERBYE* DE21 ....**3** K4
Drage St *DERBY* DE1 ....**34** C4
Draycott Cl *HEANOR* DE75 ....**9** H4
Draycott Dr *MCKLVR* DE3 ....**39** H3
Draycott Rd *BWSH/BRSTN* DE72 ...**45** H5
  BWSH/BRSTN DE72.............**57** F2
Drayton Av *DERBYW* DE22 ....**32** C5
Dresden Cl *MCKLVR* DE3 ....**39** H4
Drewry Ct *DERBYW* DE22 ....**2** A2
Drewry La *DERBYW* DE22 ....**41** H2
Dreyfus Cl *DERBYE* DE21 ....**45** E1
The Drive *BPR/DUF* DE56 ....**6** C4
Drury Av *DERBYE* DE21.................**44** C2
Dryden St *NORM/LIT* DE23 ....**52** A3
Drysdale Rd *MCKLVR* DE3.............**40** A3
Duesbury Cl *DERBYSE* DE24 ....**54** B1
Duffield Bank *BPR/DUF* DE56 ....**18** B1
Duffield Ct *BPR/DUF* * DE56 ....**17** H1
Duffield Rd *BPR/DUF* DE56 ....**18** C4
  DERBYW DE22..............................**34** A4
Dukeries La *DERBYE* DE21 ....**36** A1
Duke St *DERBY* DE1 ....**2** D1
Duluth Av *DERBYE* DE21 ....**35** H4
Dulverton Av *DERBYSE* DE24 ....**53** F1
Dulwich Rd *DERBYW* DE22............**32** B5
Dumbles La *RIPLEY* DE5 ....**9** E5
Dunbar Cl *DERBYSE* DE24 ....**61** H2
Duncan Cl *BPR/DUF* DE56 ....**6** C2
Duncan Rd *NORM/LIT* DE23 ....**52** A1
Dunedin Cl *MCKLVR* DE3...............**40** B3
Dunkery Ct *DERBYE* DE21 ....**35** F1
Dunkirk *DERBYW* DE22 ....**2** B4
Dunnicliffe La *MELB/CHEL* DE73 ...**75** H4
Dunoon Cl *DERBYSE* DE24 ....**61** H1
Dunsmore Dr *DERBYE* DE21.........**35** H1
Dunstall Park Rd
  DERBYSE DE24 ....**53** E1
Dunton Cl *DERBYE* DE21 ....**3** G3
Dunvegan Cl *DERBYSE* DE24 ....**51** A1
Durham Av *DERBYE* DE21 ....**35** F5
Durley Cl *DERBYSE* DE24...............**54** B2
Durward Cl *DERBYSE* DE24 ....**52** D2

E

Ealing Cl *DERBYW* DE22 ....**32**
Eardley Cl *DERBYE* DE21 ....**44**
Earls Crs *DERBYE* DE21 ....**36**
Earlswood Cl
  BWSH/BRSTN DE72.............**57**
Earlswood Dr *MCKLVR* DE3 ....**40**
East Av *MCKLVR* DE3 ....**40**
Eastbrae Rd *NORM/LIT* DE23 ......**51**
East Cl *DERBYW* DE22 ....**33**
East Crs *BPR/DUF* DE56 ....**12**
East Croft Av *NORM/LIT* DE23 .....**51**
East Lawn *RDERBYSW* DE65..........**60**
Eastleigh Dr *MCKLVR* DE3.............**40**
East Service Rd *DERBYE* DE21.......**44**
East St *DERBY* DE1.........................**2**
Eastway *CDON/KEG* DE74.............**73**
Eastwood Av *NORM/LIT* DE23 ......**41**
Eastwood Dr *NORM/LIT* DE23 ......**41**
Eaton Av *DERBYW* DE22 ....**26**
Eaton Bank *BPR/DUF* DE56 ....**18**
Eaton Cl *DERBYW* DE22 ....**26**
Eaton Ct *BPR/DUF* DE56 ....**17**
  DERBY DE1 ....**33**
Eaton Rd *CDON/KEG* DE74 ....**73**
Ecclesbourne Av
  BPR/DUF DE56 ....**18**
Ecclesbourne Cl *BPR/DUF* DE56 ...**17**
Edale Av *DERBYSE* DE24 ....**54**
  MCKLVR DE3 ....**40**
  NORM/LIT DE23...........................**41**
Edale Cl *DERBYW* DE22 ....**33**
Edale Dr *DERBYE* DE21 ....**45**
Eden Rd *DERBYE* DE21 ....**44**
Edensor Dr *BPR/DUF* DE56 ....**6**
Edensor Sq *DERBYW* DE22 ....**2**
Eden St *DERBYSE* DE24 ....**54**
Edgbaston Ct *NORM/LIT* DE23......**51**
Edge Hl *MELB/CHEL* DE73.............**63**
Edgelaw Ct *DERBYSE* DE24 ....**61**
Edgware Rd *DERBYW* DE22 ....**32**
Edith Wood Cl *DERBYSE* DE24 .....**54**
Edmund Rd *DERBYE* DE21 ....**45**
Ednaston Av *NORM/LIT* DE23 ......**51**
Edward Av *DERBYE* DE21 ....**43**
Edwards Crs *BPR/DUF* DE56 ....**13**
Edward St *BPR/DUF* DE56 ....**6**
  DERBY DE1 ....**2**
Edwinstowe Rd *DERBYE* DE21 .....**35**
Eggesford Rd *DERBYSE* DE24 ....**61**
Eggington Rd *RDERBYSW* DE65 ....**58**
Egmanton Rd *DERBYE* DE21 ....**36**
Egreaves Av *HEANOR* DE75 ....**9**
Eland Cl *DERBYE* DE21 ....**37**
Eley Wk *DERBY* * DE1 ....**2**
Elgin Av *NORM/LIT* DE23 ....**40**
Eliot Rd *NORM/LIT* DE23 ....**51**
Elizabeth Cl *DERBYE* DE21 ....**44**
Elkstone Cl *DERBYE* DE21 ....**36**
Ellastone Gdns *DERBYSE* DE24 ....**54**
Ellendale Rd *DERBYE* DE21 ....**36**
Ellesmere Av *DERBYSE* DE24 ....**43**
Ellison Av *BWSH/BRSTN* DE72 .....**65**
Elm Av *BPR/DUF* DE56 ....**6**
Elm Gv *DERBYE* DE21 ....**44**
  DERBYW DE22..............................**25**
Elms Av *NORM/LIT* DE23 ....**41**
Elms Dr *NORM/LIT* DE23 ....**41**
Elms Gv *RDERBYSW* DE65 ....**58**
Elms St *DERBY* DE1 ....**34**
Elm St *BWSH/BRSTN* DE72 ....**45**
Elm Tree Av *BPR/DUF* DE56 ....**13**
Elmtree Av *DERBYSE* DE24 ....**52**
Elmwood Dr *DERBYE* DE21 ....**34**
Elton Rd *DERBYSE* DE24 ....**52**
Elvaston La *DERBYSE* DE24 ....**54**
Elvaston St *BWSH/BRSTN* DE72 ...**57**
Embankment Cl *DERBYW* DE22 ....**32**
Emerald Cl *DERBYE* DE21 ....**35**
Emerson Sq *NORM/LIT* DE23 ....**52**
Empress Rd *NORM/LIT* DE23 ....**42**
Endsleigh Gdns *DERBYW* DE22 ....**32**
Enfield Rd *DERBYW* DE22 ....**33**
Ennis Cl *DERBYE* DE21..................**36**
Enoch Stone Dr *DERBYE* DE21 .....**44**
Epping Cl *DERBYW* DE22...............**32**
Epworth Dr *DERBYSE* DE24 ....**53**
Eskdale Wk *DERBYSE* * DE24 ....**54**
Essex St *DERBYE* DE21 ....**3**
Eton St *DERBYSE* DE24 ....**43**
Etruria Gdns *DERBY* DE1 ....**34**
Etta's Wy *RDERBYSW* DE65 ....**48**
Ettrick Dr *DERBYSE* DE24 ....**61**
Etwall La *RDERBYSW* DE65...........**48**
Etwall Rd *MCKLVR* DE3.................**49**

RDERBYSW DE65......................59 F5
wall St DERBYW DE22...............41 G1
ston Dr DERBY DE1...................34 C4
rans Av DERBYW DE22................26 B3
anston Gdns DERBYE DE21........36 A5
elyn Gv DERBYE DE21.................43 H1
ergreen Cl DERBYE DE21............27 H5
esham Cl DERBYE DE21..............35 F2
xcelsior Av DERBYSE DE24.........53 G3
change St DERBY DE1...................2 A3
eter Pl DERBY DE1.........................2 A4
e Eyrie DERBYSE DE24................61 H2

F

irbourne Dr MCKLVR DE3.............40 A2
irdene NORM/LIT DE23...............42 A4
ires Cl BWSH/BRSTN DE72..........46 A5
re St DERBYW DE22...................41 H3
irfax Rd NORM/LIT DE23.............42 A4
irfield Av BWSH/BRSTN DE72......45 H3
irfield Rd ILK DE7......................14 B3
NORM/LIT DE23.........................41 H4
irfield Ter
BWSH/BRSTN * DE72..................56 A1
irford Gdns NORM/LIT DE23........50 D3
irisle Cl DERBYE DE21................28 B5
irlawns NORM/LIT DE23..............17 C2
irview Cl BPR/DUF DE56..............14 A3
NORM/LIT DE23.........................50 D1
irview Gra BPR/DUF DE56...........14 A3
irway Cl DERBYW DE22..............33 G1
irway Crs DERBYW DE22.............33 G1
irwood Dr DERBYSE DE24...........54 C3
lcons Ri BPR/DUF DE56...............6 D2
lcon Wy DERBYSE DE24.............61 G2
allow Rd DERBYE DE21...............37 E5
lmouth Rd DERBYSE DE24..........54 B4
ar Cft DERBYSE DE21.................57 C1
ar La BWSH/BRSTN DE72............46 A1
ar Laund BPR/DUF DE56................6 C1
arley Rd NORM/LIT DE23.............41 G4
arm Cl BPR/DUF DE56..................6 D3
BPR/DUF DE56.............................13 G1
arm Dr DERBYSE DE24................53 H4
armhouse Ms
RDERBYSW * DE65.....................60 A2
armhouse Rd DERBYSE DE24......61 H1
armlands La NORM/LIT DE23......51 E3
arm St DERBYW DE22..................2 A7
arnah Green Rd BPR/DUF DE56.....5 C4
arnborough Gdns
DERBYW DE22.............................26 C4
arncombe La DERBYSE DE21.......27 G5
arnworth Rd MCKLVR DE3...........39 H4
arnham Cl MCKLVR DE3..............39 H4
arningham Cl DERBYE DE21........45 E1
arnway DERBYW DE22................33 H2
arrier Gdns NORM/LIT DE23........50 D2
arringdon Cl DERBYW DE22.........32 C5
aversham Cl DERBYSE DE24........53 G4
ellow Lands Wy
DERBYSE DE24.............................61 G1
MELB/CHEL DE73.........................63 H2
ellside BPR/DUF DE56..................6 B3
DERBYE DE21...............................45 E1
enchurch Wk DERBYW DE22.......33 E5
enton Rd MCKLVR DE3...............39 H4
enwick St DERBYE DE24.............53 E2
ernhill Ct MELB/CHEL DE73.........63 H1
ernwood Cl NORM/LIT DE23.......51 F1
errers Cl CDON/KEG DE74...........72 D4
errers Dr BPR/DUF DE56.............17 G2
errers Wy DERBYW DE22............33 H1
estival Av BWSH/BRSTN DE72.....57 F1
ield Cl BWSH/BRSTN DE72...........45 G3
ield Ct BPR/DUF DE56.................13 H3
ield Crs DERBYSE DE24...............53 H4
ield Dr DERBYSE DE24................53 H4
ieldfare Ct NORM/LIT DE23..........50 D3
ieldgate Dr DERBYE DE21............35 G1
ield Head Wy DERBYE DE21........28 A5
ield La BPR/DUF DE56...................6 A3
DERBYE DE21...............................35 H4
DERBYSE DE24.............................54 A3
ieldon Cl ASHB DE6....................31 E1
ield Ri NORM/LIT DE23...............51 F2
ield Rw BPR/DUF DE56.................6 A3
ieldsway Dr DERBYE DE21..........35 E1
ife St DERBYSE DE24..................53 F1
incham Cl DERBYE DE21.............35 E2
inch Crs MCKLVR DE3.................49 H1
inchley Av MCKLVR DE3..............32 C5
indern Cl BPR/DUF DE56...............6 C5
DERBYW DE22.............................33 G2
indern La RDERBYSW DE65.........49 F4

RDERBYSW DE65......................59 H5
Findern St DERBYW DE22.............41 G1
Finmere Cl NORM/LIT DE23..........50 D1
Finningley Dr DERBYW DE22.........33 H1
Finsbury Av DERBYW DE22...........33 E5
Firestone BPR/DUF DE56.............11 G2
Firfield Av BWSH/BRSTN DE72......57 H1
Firs Crs DERBYW DE22................25 H3
Firtree Gv DERBYE DE21..............36 A1
Fisher La BPR/DUF DE56..............17 H1
Fisher St DERBYSE DE24.............53 F3
Fiskerton Wy DERBYE DE21.........36 A3
Flagshaw La ASHB DE6................22 D3
Flamstead Av HEANOR DE75...........9 H5
Flamstead La RIPLEY DE5............14 C1
Flamstead St DERBYSE DE24........53 E5
The Flat BPR/DUF DE56...............13 G2
Flaxholme Av BPR/DUF DE56........18 A4
The Fleet BPR/DUF DE56................6 A5
Fleet Crs BPR/DUF DE56................6 A4
Fleet Pk BPR/DUF DE56..................6 B4
Fleet St NORM/LIT DE23...............42 B4
Flint St DERBYSE DE24.................53 E5
Flood St BWSH/BRSTN DE72.........45 H2
Folkestone Dr DERBYSE DE24.......53 H4
Folly Rd DERBYW DE22................34 C2
Ford Av HEANOR DE75...................9 H5
Ford La DERBYE DE21..................26 D3
Ford St BPR/DUF DE56...................6 A3
DERBY DE1....................................2 B3
Fordwells Cl NORM/LIT DE23........50 D1
Foremark Av NORM/LIT DE23........51 H1
Forest Cl BPR/DUF DE56................6 C2
Forester St DERBY DE1..................2 A7
Forman St DERBYW DE22...............2 B4
Forrester Av
BWSH/BRSTN DE72......................71 G2
Forty Foot La MELB/CHEL DE73.....76 D4
Forum Cl DERBYSE DE24..............54 C4
Fosbrook Dr CDON/KEG DE74........72 C5
Fosse Cl BWSH/BRSTN DE72........45 H5
Foundry La BPR/DUF DE56...........12 A3
Fountains Cl DERBYW DE22..........26 B4
Fowler Av DERBYE DE21..............44 C2
Fowler St BWSH/BRSTN DE72......57 E2
DERBYW DE22..............................33 H5
Fox Cl DERBYSE DE24..................61 G2
Foxdell Wy MELB/CHEL DE73.......64 A2
Foxes Wk DERBYW DE22.............25 H4
Foxfields Dr DERBYE DE21...........35 F1
Foxglove Dr DERBYE DE21...........27 G5
Foxlands Av DERBYW DE22..........34 A1
Foxley Ct DERBYE DE21...............35 H1
Fox Rd CDON/KEG DE74................72 C3
Fox St DERBY DE1...........................2 E1
Foyle Av DERBYE DE21................43 H2
Frampton Gdns NORM/LIT DE23....50 D3
Franchise St DERBYW DE22..........41 H2
Francis St DERBYE DE21..................3 J2
Franklyn Dr DERBYSE DE24..........53 H3
Frazer Cl DERBYE DE21................36 D5
Frederick Av DERBYSE DE24.........53 G3
Frederick St DERBYW DE22...........33 G5
Freehold St DERBYW DE22............41 H2
Freeman Av NORM/LIT DE23.........51 H3
Freemantle Rd MCKLVR DE3.........40 B3
Freesia Cl MCKLVR DE3...............40 B5
French La DERBYE DE21..............13 C5
French St NORM/LIT DE23............41 H4
Fresco Dr NORM/LIT DE23............50 C2
Freshwater Houses
DERBYW * DE22...........................54 B2
Friar Ga DERBY DE1........................2 A3
Friar Gate Ct DERBY DE1................2 A3
Friars Cl DERBYW DE22................34 A1
Friary Av DERBYSE DE24..............53 F4
Friary St DERBY DE1......................2 A4
Frizams La MELB/CHEL DE73........60 C5
Froggatt Cl DERBYW DE22............26 B3
Fulbrook Rd NORM/LIT DE23.........50 D2
Fulham Rd DERBYW DE22............40 D1
Full St DERBY DE1...........................2 B1
Fulmar Cl MCKLVR DE3................40 D3
Furnace La HEANOR DE75...............9 H3
Furrows End DERBYE DE21............28 B5

G

Gable Ct MCKLVR DE3..................50 B1
Gainsborough Cl DERBYE DE21.....36 A2
Gairloch Cl DERBYSE DE24...........61 G2
Galway Av DERBYE DE21..............44 A2
Garden Crs CDON/KEG DE74.........73 E4
Garden St DERBY DE1......................2 B1
Garfield Av BWSH/BRSTN DE72.....56 D2
Garfield Cl NORM/LIT DE23...........51 F3

Garrick St DERBYSE DE24............53 H2
Garry Cl DERBYSE DE24...............61 G2
Garth Crs DERBYSE DE24.............54 A3
Garthorpe Ct DERBYE DE21..........35 G1
Gary Cl NORM/LIT DE23...............51 G4
Gascoigne Dr DERBYE DE21.........44 C2
Gaskell Av NORM/LIT DE23..........51 H2
Gasny Av CDON/KEG DE74...........73 E2
Gatcombe Cl DERBYE DE21..........35 H1
Gayton Av NORM/LIT DE23...........51 G3
Gayton Thorpe Cl
NORM/LIT DE23...........................50 C2
Gema Cl DERBYW DE22................26 B4
George St BPR/DUF DE56................6 A3
DERBY DE1....................................2 B3
MELB/CHEL DE73.........................75 H3
Gerard Cl DERBYW DE22..............37 E5
Gerard Ct DERBY DE1.....................2 A5
Gerard Gv RDERBYSW DE65..........48 B5
Gerard St DERBY DE1......................2 B6
Gertrude Rd BWSH/BRSTN DE72....56 D2
DERBYE DE21...............................35 H3
Gibfield La BPR/DUF DE56..............6 A5
Gilbert Cl DERBYE DE21...............44 C2
Gilbert Crs BPR/DUF DE56............17 H3
Gilbert St DERBYSE DE24.............54 A4
Gilderdale Wy DERBYE DE21.........28 A5
Gillamoor Ct DERBYSE DE24.........54 C3
Gisborne Cl MCKLVR DE3.............40 B2
Gisborne Crs DERBYW DE22.........26 A4
Gisborne Gn DERBY DE1...............33 H5
Gladstone Cl MELB/CHEL DE73.....63 G1
Gladstone Rd DERBYSE DE24........53 G1
Gladstone St NORM/LIT DE23........41 H5
Glaisdale Nook DERBYSE * DE24...54 C3
Glamis Cl DERBYE DE21................36 A1
Glastonbury Rd DERBYSE DE24.....54 B2
Gleadmoss La DERBYE DE21.........35 H2
Glebe Av ILK DE7.........................15 E4
Glebe Crs ILK DE7........................29 C3
Glebe Ri NORM/LIT DE23..............41 F5
Glen Av BPR/DUF DE56.................12 C5
Glencroft Dr DERBYSE DE24..........61 G1
Glendale Dr DERBYE DE21............45 E1
Glendon Rd DERBYSE DE24..........61 G1
Glendon St ILK DE7......................21 F4
Gleneagles Cl MCKLVR DE3..........40 C4
Glenfield Crs MCKLVR DE3............39 H4
Glengarry Wy DERBYSE DE24........51 G5
Glenmore Dr DERBYSE DE24.........51 G5
Glenmoy Cl NORM/LIT DE23.........51 G2
Glenn Wy BWSH/BRSTN DE72.......56 B2
Glenorchy Cl DERBYE DE21...........28 A5
Glen Park Cl MELB/CHEL DE73......63 G4
Glen Vw BPR/DUF DE56..................6 A5
Glenwood Rd MELB/CHEL DE73.....63 H4
Glossop St DERBYSE DE24............52 C2
Gloster St DERBYSE DE24.............43 F4
Goathland Rd DERBYSE DE24........61 G2
Goldcrest Dr DERBYE DE21...........37 E5
Golden Va ILK DE7........................14 A4
Gold La DERBYW DE22.................32 B3
Goldstone Cl DERBYE DE21...........44 C2
Golf Cl NORM/LIT DE23................40 D5
Golf La BPR/DUF DE56..................11 H5
Goodale St NORM/LIT DE23..........42 B5
Goodrington Rd DERBYE DE21......28 B5
Goodsmoor Rd DERBYSE DE24......51 H4
Goods Rd BPR/DUF DE56................6 A5
Goods Yd BPR/DUF DE56..............12 A1
Goodwin's La NORM/LIT DE23.......11 F1
Goodwood Dr DERBYSE DE24........54 B3
Gordon Rd BWSH/BRSTN DE72.....45 G5
NORM/LIT DE23...........................42 A3
Gorse Cl NORM/LIT DE23.............51 E3
Gorsey Cl BPR/DUF DE56................5 H1
Gorsty Leys RDERBYSW DE65.......60 A2
Gosforth Rd DERBYSE DE24..........53 F2
Gower St DERBY DE1......................2 C5
Grafham Cl MELB/CHEL DE73.......63 H4
Grafton St NORM/LIT DE23...........41 H4
Grammer St RIPLEY DE5.................9 F3
Grampian Wy DERBYSE DE24........61 G1
Grandfield St HEANOR DE75............9 H3
Grandstand Rd DERBYE DE21..........3 H1
The Grange HEANOR DE75...............9 H3
Grange Cl MELB/CHEL DE73..........76 A2
Grange Dr CDON/KEG DE74...........72 D4
Grange Farm Cl
CDON/KEG DE74..........................73 F2
Grange Rd DERBYSE DE24............54 A4
Grange St NORM/LIT DE23............42 C4
Grangewood Dr BPR/DUF DE56.....12 B3
Grant Av DERBYE DE21................44 A1
Grantham Av DERBYE DE21..........35 F2
Granville Cl BPR/DUF DE56...........17 H3

Granville St DERBY DE1................41 H1
Grasmere Av DERBYE DE21..........36 D5
Grasmere Crs DERBYSE DE24.......51 H5
Grassthorpe Cl DERBYE DE21.......36 A2
Grassy La RDERBYSW DE65..........49 F2
Gravel Pit La DERBYE DE21..........44 D2
Grayling St DERBY DE1.................42 C4
Great Northern Rd DERBY DE1......41 H1
Greatorex Av DERBYSE DE24........53 F4
The Green ASHB DE6....................30 B2
BWSH/BRSTN DE72......................65 C5
CDON/KEG DE74..........................72 D4
DERBYW DE22..............................33 G2
MCKLVR DE3...............................40 A5
RDERBYSW DE65.........................60 A3
Greenacres NORM/LIT DE23.........51 E1
Green Av MELB/CHEL DE73...........63 H3
Greenbank DERBYE DE21.............44 C2
Greenburn Cl NORM/LIT DE23.......51 F3
Greenfields Av NORM/LIT DE23.....51 E2
Greenfinch Cl DERBYE DE21.........37 E5
Greenland Av DERBYW DE22.........41 E1
Green La BPR/DUF DE56.................6 A3
BWSH/BRSTN DE72......................45 H1
DERBY DE1....................................2 C5
DERBYSE DE24.............................54 B1
MELB/CHEL DE73.........................68 B3
MELB/CHEL DE73.........................76 D5
RDERBYSW DE65.........................49 G5
Green Leas BWSH/BRSTN DE72....65 F4
Greenmount Cl NORM/LIT DE23....50 D3
Green Pk DERBYW DE22...............32 D5
Greenside Cl MCKLVR DE3...........39 H4
The Greenway DERBYSE DE24......54 C4
Green Wy RDERBYSW DE65..........60 A2
Greenway Cl
BWSH/BRSTN DE72......................45 G3
Greenway Dr NORM/LIT DE23.......40 D5
Greenwich Dr North
DERBYW DE22..............................41 E1
Greenwich Dr South
DERBYW DE22..............................40 D1
Greenwood Av DERBYE DE21........35 C3
Greenwood Cl DERBYSE DE24.......53 E4
Gregory Av BWSH/BRSTN DE72....57 F1
Gregorys Wy BPR/DUF DE56..........6 D2
Grendon Cl BPR/DUF DE56.............6 C1
Grenfell Av NORM/LIT DE23..........51 H3
Gresham Rd DERBYSE DE24..........52 D1
Grey St DERBYW DE22....................2 B6
Griffin Cl DERBYSE DE24..............53 G2
Grimshaw Av DERBYSE DE24........54 A2
Grindlow Rd DERBYE DE21...........35 H3
Groombridge Crs
NORM/LIT DE23...........................50 D3
Groome Av HEANOR DE75...............9 H3
Grosvenor Dr NORM/LIT DE23.......50 D3
Grosvenor St DERBYSE DE24........42 D5
The Grove MCKLVR DE3...............40 B4
Grove Bank DERBY * DE1.............34 A4
Grovebury Dr NORM/LIT DE23.......51 F4
Grove Cl BWSH/BRSTN DE72........55 E5
Grove Pk RDERBYSW DE65............58 A2
Groves Nook MELB/CHEL DE73......63 F3
Grove St NORM/LIT DE23.............42 B3
Gunhills La BPR/DUF DE56............10 B4
Gurney Av NORM/LIT DE23...........51 C3
Gypsy La BWSH/BRSTN DE72.......56 B1

H

Haddon Cl DERBYW DE22.............25 G5
Haddon Dr DERBYE DE21.............45 E2
DERBYW DE22..............................25 G5
MCKLVR DE3...............................40 B3
Haddon St NORM/LIT DE23...........41 H5
Haig St DERBYSE DE24................53 G1
Hailsham Cl MCKLVR DE3.............40 A4
Haines Cl DERBYSE DE24.............52 A5
Hallam Flds CDON/KEG DE74........73 E5
Hall Dyke DERBYE DE21...............44 D1
Hall Farm Cl DERBY DE1..............72 D4
Hall Farm Rd BPR/DUF DE56........17 H3
Hallgate Cl DERBYE DE21.............28 B5
Hall Leys La MELB/CHEL DE73......76 D1
Hall Pk MELB/CHEL DE73.............68 B2
Hall Park Cl NORM/LIT DE23.........41 E5
Hall St DERBYSE DE24..................53 H2
Halstock Dr DERBYSE DE24...........54 B1
Hambledon Dr DERBYSE DE24......61 G2
Hamblin Crs DERBYSE DE24.........52 A5
Hamilton Cl MCKLVR DE3.............40 C3
Hamilton Rd DERBYE DE21...........37 E5
NORM/LIT DE23...........................42 A4
Hampden St NORM/LIT DE23.........52 B1
Hampshire Rd DERBYE DE21.........34 D3

Hampstead Dr *DERBYW* DE22 ....**32** D5
Hampton Cl *DERBY* DE21 ....**45** E1
Hanbury Rd *DERBYE* DE21 ....**35** F5
Handel St *DERBYSE* DE24 ....**52** D1
Handford Ct *DERBY * DE22 ....**41** G1
Handford St *DERBY* DE22 ....**41** G1
Handyside St *DERBY* DE1 ....**2** C1
Hanger Bank
   BWSH/BRSTN DE72 ....**65** G4
Hanover Sq *DERBYW* DE22 ....**32** D5
Hansard Ga *DERBY* DE1 ....**3** G3
Hanslynn *BWSH/BRSTN* DE72 ....**55** E5
Hanwell Wy *DERBYW* DE22 ......**33** E5
Harcourt Pl *CDON/KEG* DE74 .....**73** E3
Harcourt St *DERBY* DE1 ....**2** B6
Hardacre Cl *MELB/CHEL* DE73 .....**75** H2
Hardhurst Rd *DERBYSE* DE24 .....**54** A4
Hardwick Av *DERBYSE* DE24 ......**25** C5
Hardwick Dr *MCKLVR* DE3 ....**40** B4
Hardwick St *DERBYSE* DE24 ......**52** D1
Harepit Cl *DERBYE* DE21 ....**27** H5
Harewood Cl *BPR/DUF* DE56 ....**7** E2
Harewood Rd *DERBYSE* DE24 ......**25** C5
Hargrave Av *BWSH/BRSTN* DE72 ..**45** H1
Hargreaves Cl *NORM/LIT* DE23 ...**50** D3
Harlech Cl *DERBYW* DE22 ....**45** F1
Harlesden Av *DERBYW* DE22 ......**32** D4
Harlow Cl *DERBYSE* DE24 ....**53** C5
Harpswell Cl *DERBYW* DE22 ....**33** H1
Harpur Av *NORM/LIT* DE23 ....**51** G2
Harrier Cl *DERBYSE* DE24 ....**61** H1
Harrier Rd *BPR/DUF* DE56 ....**6** D2
Harrier Wy *DERBYSE* DE24 ....**61** H1
Harriet St *NORM/LIT* DE23 ....**42** B3
Harringay Gdns *DERBYW* DE22 ...**33** F5
Harrington Av
   BWSH/BRSTN DE72 ....**45** H4
Harrington Rd *NORM/LIT* DE23 ...**41** F5
Harrington St
   BWSH/BRSTN DE72 ....**57** E2
   DERBYSE DE24 ....**53** F3
   NORM/LIT DE23 ....**52** B1
Harrison St *DERBYW* DE22 ....**41** H3
Harrogate Crs *DERBYE* DE21 ......**35** E2
Harrow St *DERBYSE* DE24 ....**43** F4
Hartington St *NORM/LIT* DE23 .....**2** D7
Hartington Wy *MCKLVR* DE3 ......**40** A4
Hartland Dr *NORM/LIT* DE23 ......**51** G3
Hartshorne Rd *NORM/LIT* DE23 ...**51** H4
Harvest Wy *DERBYE* DE21 ....**28** B5
Harvey Rd *CDON/KEG* DE74 ....**73** E5
   DERBYSE DE24 ....**53** F3
Hasgill Cl *DERBYE* DE21 ....**28** B5
Haslam's La *DERBYW* DE22 ....**34** B1
Haslemere Cl *NORM/LIT* DE23 ....**42** C4
Hassop Rd *DERBYE* DE21 ....**35** H3
Hastings St *CDON/KEG* DE74 .....**73** E5
   NORM/LIT DE23 ....**42** B5
Hatchmere Cl *DERBYE* DE21 ......**35** H2
Hatfield Rd *DERBYSE* DE24 ....**53** G4
Hathern Cl *NORM/LIT* DE23 ....**51** H4
Hathersage Av *NORM/LIT* DE23 ..**51** H1
Hatton Ct *MELB/CHEL* DE73 ......**75** H4
Haulton Dr *CDON/KEG* DE74 ......**72** D3
Havelock Rd *NORM/LIT* DE23 .....**52** A1
Haven Baulk Av *NORM/LIT* DE23 ..**50** B2
Haven Baulk La *MCKLVR* DE3 .....**50** A2
Haven Ct *DERBYSE* DE24 ....**54** C3
Hawke St *DERBYW* DE22 ....**41** F1
Hawksdale Cl *MELB/CHEL* DE73 ...**63** H3
Hawkshead Av *DERBYE* DE21 .....**35** E2
Hawthorn Av *DERBYSE* DE24 ......**43** F4
Hawthorn Crs *RDERBYSW* DE65 ...**60** A2
Hawthorne Av
   BWSH/BRSTN DE72 ....**45** G3
Hawthorne Cl *BPR/DUF* DE56 ....**7** C5
The Hawthornes
   *BPR/DUF * DE56 ....**7** E2
Hawthorn Rd *CDON/KEG* DE74 ...**73** E2
The Hawthorns *DERBYE* DE21 .....**18** D5
Hawthorn St *DERBYSE* DE24 ......**52** D1
Hawtrey Gdns *DERBYSE* DE24 ....**53** H3
Haydn Rd *DERBYE* DE21 ....**35** G3
Haydock Park Rd
   DERBYSE DE24 ....**53** F1
The Hayes *RDERBYSW* DE65 ......**59** H3
Hayes Av *BWSH/BRSTN* DE72 ....**57** E2
   NORM/LIT DE23 ....**51** G1
Hayes Wood Rd *ILK* DE7 ....**21** G4
Hayfield Cl *BPR/DUF* DE56 ....**6** C2
Hayley Cft *BPR/DUF* DE56 ....**18** A4
Haywood Cl *DERBYSE* DE24 ......**53** H4
Hazel Av *NORM/LIT* DE23 ....**51** G3
Hazel Cl *RDERBYSW* DE65 ....**60** A2
Hazeldene Cl *BPR/DUF* DE56 ......**11** H5
Hazel Dr *DERBYE* DE21 ....**37** F5
Hazel Gv *BPR/DUF* DE56 ....**17** H2

Hazelrigg Cl *CDON/KEG* DE74 .....**72** C3
Hazelwood Hl *BPR/DUF* DE56 .....**11** E2
Hazelwood Rd *BPR/DUF* DE56 ....**11** F3
   DERBYE DE21 ....**35** G3
Headingley St *NORM/LIT* DE23 ...**51** F1
Heage La *RDERBYSW* DE65 ....**48** B2
Heanor Gate Rd *HEANOR* DE75 ...**15** H1
Heanor Houses *DERBYE * DE21 ....**44** D3
Heanor Rd *ILK* DE7 ....**15** F3
   RIPLEY DE5 ....**9** F4
Heath Av *NORM/LIT* DE23 ....**41** F4
Heathcote Cl *DERBYSE* DE24 ......**54** B4
Heath Ct *DERBYSE* DE24 ....**61** H1
Heather Cl *DERBYSE* DE24 ....**61** G2
Heather Crs *NORM/LIT* DE23 ......**51** F3
Heathermead Cl *DERBYSE* DE24 ..**35** G2
Heath La *RDERBYSW* DE65 ....**60** A4
Hebden Cl *NORM/LIT* DE23 ....**50** C3
Hebrides Cl *DERBYSE* DE24 ....**61** G1
Hedgebank Ct *DERBYE* DE21 ......**28** B5
Hedgerow Gdns *DERBYE* DE21 ...**28** B5
Hedingham Wy *MCKLVR* DE3 .....**49** H1
Heigham Ct *DERBYSE* DE24 ....**63** E1
Helston Cl *DERBYSE* DE24 ....**54** A3
Hemington Hl *CDON/KEG* DE74 ...**73** G3
Hemington La *CDON/KEG* DE74 ...**73** H2
Hemlock Cl *DERBYE* DE21 ....**27** H5
Hendon Wy *DERBYW* DE22 ....**33** E5
Henry St *DERBY* DE1 ....**2** B1
Hereford Rd *DERBYE* DE21 ....**35** E3
Hermitage Av
   BWSH/BRSTN DE72 ....**45** H4
Hermitage Ct *DERBYSE* DE24 .....**36** A2
Heronswood Dr *DERBYE* DE21 ....**36** B5
Heron Wy *MCKLVR* DE3 ....**40** D4
Heydon Cl *BPR/DUF* DE56 ....**6** C1
Heyworth St *DERBYW* DE22 ......**33** F5
Hickling Cl *DERBYSE* DE24 ....**63** E1
High Bank *RIPLEY* DE5 ....**9** E5
Highbury Cl *DERBYW* DE22 ....**32** C5
Highfield Cl *HEANOR* DE75 ....**9** G2
Highfield Cottages
   *DERBYE * DE21 ....**43** F1
Highfield Gdns *DERBYW* DE22 ....**34** A3
Highfield La *DERBYE* DE21 ....**43** F1
Highfield Ms *DERBYE * DE21 ....**43** F1
Highfield Rd *BPR/DUF* DE56 ....**6** A5
   BPR/DUF DE56 ....**13** G2
   DERBYE DE21 ....**26** D1
   DERBYW DE22 ....**34** A4
   NORM/LIT DE23 ....**51** F2
Highgates *DERBY * DE1 ....**2** D6
High Gv *BPR/DUF* DE56 ....**7** E3
Highgrove Dr *MELB/CHEL* DE73 ...**63** G2
High Pavement *BPR/DUF * DE56 ....**6** B4
High St *BPR/DUF* DE56 ....**6** B4
   BPR/DUF DE56 ....**13** H2
   CDON/KEG DE74 ....**72** D5
   HEANOR DE75 ....**9** H3
   MELB/CHEL DE73 ....**63** H3
   MELB/CHEL DE73 ....**75** H5
Highwood Av *BPR/DUF* DE56 ....**12** C1
High Wood Bank
   BPR/DUF DE56 ....**12** D1
Hilary Cl *BPR/DUF* DE56 ....**7** F2
Hilderstone Cl *DERBYSE* DE24 ....**54** C3
The Hill *DERBYW* DE22 ....**34** B2
Hill Brow *DERBY* DE1 ....**2** C5
Hill Cl *DERBYE* DE21 ....**44** D2
   ILK DE7 ....**21** F4
Hillcrest Dr *BPR/DUF* DE56 ....**13** H2
Hillcreste Dr *MELB/CHEL* DE73 ...**63** G1
Hill Crest Rd *DERBYE* DE21 ....**35** E4
Hill Croft Dr *BWSH/BRSTN* DE72 ..**45** H2
Hill Cross Av *NORM/LIT* DE23 ....**51** F2
Hill Cross Dr *NORM/LIT* DE23 ....**51** G2
Hill Rise Cl *NORM/LIT* DE23 ......**51** G2
Hillside *RDERBYSW* DE65 ....**60** A2
Hillside Av *DERBYE* DE21 ....**43** H1
Hillside Crs *DERBYE* DE21 ....**44** D2
Hillside Ri *BPR/DUF* DE56 ....**6** A5
Hillside Rd *DERBYE* DE21 ....**44** D2
Hills Rd *BWSH/BRSTN* DE72 ......**57** E1
Hillsway *MELB/CHEL* DE73 ....**63** G1
   NORM/LIT DE23 ....**41** E5
Hilltop Derbye DE21 ....**35** E1
Hilltop La *BPR/DUF* DE56 ....**7** F5
Hill Vw *BPR/DUF* DE56 ....**17** G2
Hill View *ILK* DE7 ....**14** A3
Hill View Gv *DERBYE* DE21 ....**44** D1
Hilton Cl *MCKLVR* DE3 ....**40** A5
Hilton Rd *RDERBYSW* DE65 ....**48** B3
Hind Av *BPR/DUF* DE56 ....**57** F2
Hindscarth Crs *MCKLVR* DE3 ......**40** B5
Hobart Cl *MCKLVR* DE3 ....**40** C4
Hob Hl *BPR/DUF* DE56 ....**11** E2
Hodge Beck Cl *DERBYSE* DE24 ...**54** B3

Hodthorpe Cl *DERBYE* DE21 ......**35** H2
Holborn Dr *DERBYW* DE22 ....**32** D4
Holbrook Rd *DERBYSE* DE24 ......**54** A3
   DERBYE DE24 ....**54** A3
Holbrook Vw *BPR/DUF* DE56 .....**13** H2
Holcombe St *NORM/LIT* DE23 ....**42** C5
Holden Av *BWSH/BRSTN* DE72 ...**65** F4
Holderness Cl *DERBYSE* DE24 ....**61** G2
Hollies Farm Cl
   *MELB/CHEL * DE73 ....**69** E4
Hollies Rd *DERBYW* DE22 ....**25** G5
Hollington Cl *DERBYE* DE21 ....**35** H4
Hollis St *DERBYSE* DE24 ....**53** H1
The Hollow *CDON/KEG* DE74 .....**73** E3
   MCKLVR DE3 ....**50** A1
   NORM/LIT DE23 ....**41** E5
Holloway Rd *BPR/DUF* DE56 ......**17** G1
   DERBYSE DE24 ....**53** G3
Hollow Brooks *DERBYE* DE21 .....**26** D1
Hollowood Av *NORM/LIT* DE23 ...**51** F1
Holly Bush La *BPR/DUF* DE56 .....**12** B4
Holly Cl *BWSH/BRSTN* DE72 ......**56** D2
Holly Ct *BWSH/BRSTN* DE72 .....**65** F5
   MCKLVR DE3 ....**40** A5
Holly House La *BPR/DUF* DE56 .....**5** F3
Hollymoor Dr *MELB/CHEL* DE73 ..**63** F2
Holm Av *DERBYE* DE21 ....**26** C1
Holme La *DERBYE* DE21 ....**44** B4
Holmesfield Dr *MCKLVR* DE3 .....**40** C4
Holmes Rd *BWSH/BRSTN* DE72 ...**57** C1
Holmes St *NORM/LIT* DE23 ....**42** B4
Holmfield *NORM/LIT* DE23 ....**51** F3
Holmoak Cl *DERBYE* DE21 ....**28** A5
Holt Av *BPR/DUF* DE56 ....**54** B3
Holtlands Dr *DERBYSE* DE24 ......**53** G4
Holyhead Dr *DERBYE* DE21 ....**36** A1
Holyrood Cl *DERBYE* DE21 ....**45** E1
Homefarm Cl
   BWSH/BRSTN DE72 ....**45** H1
Home Farm Dr *DERBYW* DE22 ...**26** B4
Honeycroft Cl *BPR/DUF* DE56 ......**6** C5
Hope Av *MCKLVR* DE3 ....**40** A4
Hope St *DERBY* DE1 ....**2** E5
   MELB/CHEL DE73 ....**75** G3
Hopetoun St *NORM/LIT* DE23 ....**52** B2
Hopping Hl *BPR/DUF* DE56 ....**12** A2
Hopton Cl *DERBYE* DE21 ....**35** G1
Hopwell Rd *BWSH/BRSTN* DE72 ..**46** D5
Hornbeam Cl *DERBYE* DE21 ....**35** F1
Horncastle Rd *DERBYE* DE21 .....**35** F1
Hornsea Rd *DERBYE* DE21 ....**35** E2
The Horse Shoes
   CDON/KEG DE74 ....**73** F3
Horsley Crs *BPR/DUF* DE56 ....**12** D3
Horsley La *DERBYE* DE21 ....**19** F1
Horsley Rd *DERBYE* DE21 ....**13** C4
Horton St *NORM/LIT* DE23 ....**42** D4
Horwood Av *NORM/LIT* DE23 ....**41** G4
Hospital La *MCKLVR* DE3 ....**49** G2
Houghton Ct *DERBYE* DE21 ....**35** C1
Hoult St *DERBYW* DE22 ....**41** G2
Hounslow Rd *DERBYW* DE22 .....**33** G5
Hoveton Cl *DERBYE* DE21 ....**63** E1
Howard St *NORM/LIT* DE23 ......**42** A4
Howden Cl *MCKLVR* DE3 ....**39** H5
Howe St *DERBYW* DE22 ....**41** G1
Howth Cl *DERBYE* DE21 ....**43** H2
Hoylake Cl *MCKLVR* DE3 ....**39** H3
Hoylake Dr *MCKLVR* DE3 ....**39** H3
Hoyland Ct *BPR/DUF* DE56 ....**7** F2
Hubert Shaw Cl *DERBYSE* DE24 ..**53** F5
Hucklow Ct *DERBYE* DE21 ....**28** A5
Hudson Wy *DERBYSE* DE24 ....**3** H7
Hulland St *DERBY* DE1 ....**3** G1
Hulland Vw *DERBYW* DE22 ....**33** G2
Humber Cl *DERBYSE* DE24 ....**54** B3
Humbleton Dr *DERBYW* DE22 ....**40** D1
Hunter Dr *BPR/DUF* DE56 ....**13** G2
Hunter Rd *BPR/DUF* DE56 ....**7** E2
Hunters Cft *DERBYSE* DE24 ......**61** H2
Huntingdon Ct
   MELB/CHEL DE73 ....**76** A2
Huntingdon Dr *CDON/KEG* DE74 ..**72** D3
Huntingdon Gn *DERBYE* DE21 ......**3** H2
Huntley Av *DERBYE* DE21 ....**37** F5
Hurst Dr *ILK* DE7 ....**29** H3
Hutton St *DERBYSE* DE24 ....**53** F3
Huxley Cl *NORM/LIT* DE23 ....**52** A2
Hyde Park Rd *DERBYW* DE22 ....**32** D5

I

Ibsley Cl *DERBYSE* DE24 ....**54** B3
Ilford Rd *DERBYW* DE22 ....**40** D1
Ilkeston Rd *ILK* DE7 ....**20** D3

Imperial Ct *DERBYW* DE22 ....**25** C
Industrial St *NORM/LIT * DE23 ....**42** B
Ingham Dr *MCKLVR* DE3 ....**50** A
Ingleby Av *NORM/LIT* DE23 ......**52** A
Ingleby La *MELB/CHEL* DE73 .....**74** E
Ingle Cl *DERBYE* DE21 ....**44** C
Ingledew Cl *DERBYE* DE21 ....**35** F
Ingle's Channel *BPR/DUF* DE56 .....**6** A
Inglewood Av *MCKLVR* DE3 ......**40** A
Ingliston Cl *DERBYSE* DE24 ....**54** C
Inn La *DERBYW* DE22 ....**25** E
Instow Dr *NORM/LIT* DE23 ....**51** C
Inveraray Cl *DERBYSE* DE24 ......**61** C
Invernia Cl *NORM/LIT* DE23 ......**51** H
Iona Cl *DERBYSE* DE24 ....**51** H
Ireton Houses *BPR/DUF * DE56 .....**7** F
Iron Ga *DERBY* DE1 ....**2** C
Irvine Cl *DERBYSE* DE24 ....**61** C
Irving Pl *DERBYSE* DE24 ....**53** C
Islay Rd *DERBYSE* DE24 ....**51** H
Isleworth Dr *DERBYW* DE22 ......**32** C
Ismay Rd *DERBYE* DE21 ....**35** C
Ivybridge Cl *DERBYE* DE21 ....**28** B
Ivy Sq *NORM/LIT* DE23 ....**42** D

J

Jacksdale Cl *DERBYW* DE22 ....**33** C
Jackson Av *MCKLVR* DE3 ....**40** D
Jacksons La *BPR/DUF* DE56 ....**11** H
   RDERBYSW DE65 ....**58** B
Jackson St *DERBYW* DE22 ....**41** H
James Cl *DERBY* DE1 ....**41** H
Jardine Ct *BWSH/BRSTN* DE72 ...**57** E
Jarvey's La *DERBYW* DE22 ....**32** B
Jarvis Rd *DERBYSE* DE24 ....**61** H
Jasmine Cl *DERBYE* DE21 ....**44** A
Jawbone La *MELB/CHEL* DE73 ....**76** B
Jedburgh Cl *DERBYSE* DE24 ......**61** H
Jefferson Pl *DERBYSE* DE24 ......**53** C
Jemison Cl *NORM/LIT* DE23 ......**50** B
Jenny's Ct *BPR/DUF* DE56 ....**6** D
Jesop Dr *DERBYSE* DE24 ....**61** H
Jodrell Av *BPR/DUF* DE56 ....**7** E
John Berrysford Cl
   DERBYE DE21 ....**43** G
John F Kennedy Gdns
   DERBYE DE21 ....**36** B
John Lombe Dr *DERBY* DE1 ......**34** B
John O'Gaunts Wy
   BPR/DUF DE56 ....**7** E
John Port Cl *RDERBYSW* DE65 ...**48** B
Johnson Av *DERBYSE* DE24 ......**53** F
John St *DERBY* DE1 ....**3** F
Joseph St *BPR/DUF* DE56 ....**6** A
   NORM/LIT DE23 ....**42** B
Joseph Wright Ter *DERBY * DE1 ..**34** B
Jubalton Cl *DERBYSE* DE24 ....**53** F
Jubilee Cl *MELB/CHEL* DE73 .....**76** A
Jubilee Ct *BPR/DUF* DE56 ....**6** B
Jubilee Rd *DERBYSE* DE24 ....**53** F
Junction Cl *DERBYSE* DE1 ....**41** G
Jury St *DERBY* DE1 ....**2** B

K

Kean Pl *DERBYSE* DE24 ....**53** E
Keats Av *NORM/LIT* DE23 ....**40** B
Keble Cl *DERBY* DE1 ....**42** C
Kedleston Cl *DERBYW* DE22 ......**33** G
Kedleston Gdns *DERBY * DE1 ......**2** B
Kedleston Old Rd
   DERBYW DE22 ....**33** G
Kedleston Rd *DERBYW* DE22 .....**24** A
   DERBYW DE22 ....**25** F
Kedleston St *DERBY* DE1 ....**2** A
Kegworth Av *NORM/LIT* DE23 ....**51** F
Keldholme La *DERBYSE* DE24 ....**54** B
Kelmoor Rd *DERBYSE* DE24 ......**54** A
Kelvedon Dr *NORM/LIT* DE23 ....**50** D
Kemble Pl *DERBYSE* DE24 ....**53** G
Kempton Park Rd
   DERBYSE DE24 ....**53** E
Kendon Av *NORM/LIT* DE23 ......**51** H
Kendray Cl *BPR/DUF* DE56 ....**7** E
Kenilworth Av *NORM/LIT* DE23 ..**52** A
Kennedy Cl *DERBYE* DE21 ....**35** H
Kensal Ri *DERBYW* DE22 ....**33** E
Kensington St *HEANOR* DE75 ....**15** H
Kensington St *DERBYW* DE22 ......**2** A
Kentish Ct *DERBY* DE1 ....**34** C
Kent St *DERBYE* DE21 ....**35** E
Kernel Cl *NORM/LIT* DE23 ....**50** D
Kerry Dr *ILK* DE7 ....**15** E

erry St *DERBYE* DE21 ....35 E4
erry's Yd *BPR/DUF* DE56 ....13 G2
ershope Dr *DERBYE* DE21 ....28 A5
estrel Cl *MCKLVR* * DE3...........49 F2
estrels Cft *DERBYW* DE22.........61 G1
evin Cl *DERBYE* DE21 ....36 A3
ew Gdns *DERBYW* DE22...........41 E1
eyhaven Cl *DERBYE* DE21 ....35 E3
eynsham Cl *DERBYSE* DE24 ......53 F1
eys St *DERBY* DE1 ....2 E2
ibworth Cl *DERBYE* DE21 ....36 A3
ilburn Cl *DERBYE* DE56 ....7 E4
ilburn Rd *BPR/DUF* DE56 ....6 D3
ildare Rd *DERBYE* DE21 ....44 A2
illingworth Av *DERBYSE* DE24....52 A5
illis La *BPR/DUF* DE56 ....13 E2
ilnsey Cl *NORM/LIT* DE23 ....50 C3
imberley Rd
       BWSH/BRSTN DE72............45 G4
inder Wk *DERBYW* * DE22 ....41 F2
ing Alfred St *DERBY* DE1 ....2 A5
ingfisher Cl *MCKLVR* DE3 ....49 G2
ingsbury Rd *DERBYW* DE22.......32 D5
ingsclere Av *DERBYE* DE21 ......15 H1
ings Cl *HEANOR* DE75 ....15 H1
ings Cft *DERBYW* DE22.............26 A4
ingsdale Gv *MELB/CHEL* DE73...63 G4
ings Dr *MCKLVR* DE3 ....41 E4
ingsland St *DERBYW* DE22........35 G1
ingsley Rd *DERBYW* DE22.........25 G5
ingsley St *DERBYSE* DE24 ....52 A4
ings Mead Cl *DERBY* DE1 ....2 B1
ingsmead Wk *DERBY* DE1 ....2 A1
ing's Mill La
       BWSH/BRSTN DE72............71 E3
ingsmuir Rd *MCKLVR* DE3 ....39 H3
ingston St *DERBY* DE1 ....34 A4
ing St *BPR/DUF* DE56 ....6 A4
       BPR/DUF DE56 ....17 H1
       DERBY DE1 ....2 B1
ingsway *DERBYW* DE22 ....33 E5
ingsway Crs *BPR/DUF* DE56 ......13 H2
ingsway Park Cl
       DERBYW DE22.................41 F1
ingswood Av *BPR/DUF* DE56 ......6 D2
inross Dr *DERBYE* DE21 ....34 D3
intyre Dr *DERBYSE* DE24 ....61 G1
ipling Dr *MCKLVR* DE3..............40 A5
irk Dale Cl *DERBYE* DE21 ....45 E3
irkfield Dr *BWSH/BRSTN* DE72....57 G1
irkistown Cl *DERBYSE* DE24 ......54 B3
irkland Cl *CDON/KEG* DE74........72 C4
irkland Wy *DERBYSE* DE24 ....61 G1
irkley Dr *HEANOR* DE75 ....15 H1
irk Leys Av North
       DERBYE DE21 ....44 D2
irk Leys Av South
       DERBYE DE21 ....44 D2
irkman Rd *HEANOR* DE75..........9 H3
irk's La *BPR/DUF* DE56.............6 C4
irkstead Cl *DERBYE* DE21 ....36 A2
irk St *DERBY* DE1 ....34 B3
itchener Av *NORM/LIT* DE23 .....52 A2
nightsbridge *DERBYW* DE22 ......32 D5
nights Cl *DERBYSE* DE24...........61 H5
noll Cl *NORM/LIT* DE23 ....50 D1
nowl Av *BPR/DUF* DE56 ....5 F1
yle Gv *DERBYE* DE21 ....28 A5
ynance Cl *DERBYSE* DE24.........54 B4

L

aburnum Crs *DERBYW* DE22 ......25 G3
aburnum Gv *DERBYW* DE22 ....40 D1
adbroke Gdns *DERBYW* DE22 ....32 C5
adybank Rd *MCKLVR* DE3 ....39 H3
adybower Rd *DERBYE* DE21 ......45 E2
adycroft Paddock
       DERBYW DE22.................25 H4
adygrove Cottages
       NORM/LIT DE23 ....42 C3
adygrove Ter *DERBYSE* * DE24 ...53 H2
ady La *RIPLEY* DE5 ....14 C1
ady Lea Hl *DERBYSE* DE24 ....13 H5
ady Lea Rd *ILK* DE7 ....13 H4
ady Mantle Cl
       MELB/CHEL DE73..............63 F2
adysmith Rd
       BWSH/BRSTN DE72............45 G4
ake Av *HEANOR* DE75 ....9 H3
ake Dr *NORM/LIT* DE24 ....52 A1
akeside Dr *NORM/LIT* DE23 ......52 A1
ambhouse La *BPR/DUF* DE56 .....4 B2
ambley Dr *DERBYW* DE22.........33 F1

Lambourn Cl *DERBYW* DE22.......26 B5
Lambourn Dr *DERBYW* DE22 ......26 B4
Lambrook Cl *MCKLVR* DE3 ....39 H4
Lampad Cl *MELB/CHEL* DE73......75 H4
Lampeter Cl *DERBYE* DE21.........36 A1
Lanark St *DERBY* DE21 ....35 F4
Lancaster Wk *DERBYE* DE21 ......37 F5
Lander La *BPR/DUF* DE56...........6 B3
Langdale Dr *DERBYE* DE21.........35 E1
Langford Rd *MCKLVR* DE3 ....40 A3
Langley Rd *DERBYE* DE21..........44 D3
Langley St *DERBYW* DE22..........41 G1
Lang Rd *DERBYSE* DE24 ....53 G3
Langsett Dr *MELB/CHEL* DE73.....63 H2
Lanscombe Park Rd
       DERBYW DE22.................33 H2
Lansdowne Av *DERBYSE* DE24....53 G4
Lansing Gdns *DERBYSE* DE24 .....36 A5
Lapwing Cl *DERBYSE* DE24 ....61 H2
Larch Cl *DERBYSE* DE24............25 C5
Larch Rd *BPR/DUF* DE56 ....14 A3
Larges St *DERBY* DE1 ....41 H1
Lark St *NORM/LIT* DE23 ....51 F3
Larkhill Crs *DERBYSE* DE24 ....52 A5
Larkspur Ct *DERBYE* DE21.........27 H5
Lashley Gdns *DERBYSE* DE24 .....35 G1
Lathbury Cl *DERBYE* DE21 ....35 E2
Lathkill Av *DERBYSE* DE24 ....54 B2
Lathkill Dr *RIPLEY* DE5 ....8 C1
Lathkill Rd *DERBYE* DE21 ....35 G3
Latimer Cl *NORM/LIT* DE23 ....50 B2
Latimer St *DERBYSE* DE24 ....53 E3
Latrigg Cl *MCKLVR* DE3 ....40 B5
Lauder Cl *DERBYSE* DE24 ....61 G1
Launceston Rd *DERBYSE* DE24 ...54 A4
Laund Av *BPR/DUF* DE56 ....6 C1
Laund Cl *BPR/DUF* DE56 ....6 C1
Laund Hl *BPR/DUF* DE56............6 C1
Laund Nook *BPR/DUF* DE56........6 B2
Laurel Bank *NORM/LIT* * DE23.....52 A1
Laurel Crs *ILK* DE7 ....15 E5
Laurel Dr *BWSH/BRSTN* DE72.....65 F5
Laurie Pl *DERBYSE* DE24 ....53 F2
Lavender Rw *DERBYW* DE22 ......34 A2
Laverstoke Ct *DERBYSE* DE24.....41 H2
Lawn Av *DERBYW* DE22.............33 G4
       RDERBYSW DE65...............48 B4
Lawn Heads Av *NORM/LIT* DE23 ...41 F4
Lawnlea Cl *NORM/LIT* DE23 ....51 H4
Lawnside *BWSH/BRSTN* DE72 .....45 E1
Lawnswood Cl *NORM/LIT* DE23....51 F1
Lawrence Av
       BWSH/BRSTN DE72............57 G1
       DERBYW DE22.................36 A4
Lawrence St *NORM/LIT* DE23 .....52 A1
Lea Cl *DERBYW* DE22...............25 H5
Leacroft Rd *NORM/LIT* DE23 ......42 C5
Lea Dr *DERBYW* DE22 ....35 G5
       MCKLVR DE3 ....40 B3
Leafenden Cl *DERBYW* DE22......34 B1
Leafgreen Cl *NORM/LIT* DE23 .....51 F3
Leafgreen La *NORM/LIT* DE23 .....51 F1
Leake St *DERBYW* DE22 ....41 G1
Leamington Cl *NORM/LIT* DE23 ...51 F3
Leander Cl *NORM/LIT* DE23 ....51 G2
Leaper St *DERBY* DE1 ....33 H5
Leawood Gdns *DERBYE* DE21 .....28 A5
Leche Cft *DERBYSE* DE56 ....7 E3
Ledbury Cha *DERBYSE* DE24.......61 G2
Leeds Pl *DERBY* DE1 ....3 G6
Lee Farm Cl *MELB/CHEL* DE73 ...63 H2
The Lees *DERBYSE* DE24 ....54 C5
Leeway *DERBYE* DE21 ....44 C2
Leicester St *DERBY* DE21..........41 H3
Leman St *DERBYW* DE22...........41 H3
Leniscar Av *HEANOR* DE75 ....9 H3
Lens Rd *DERBYW* DE22.............33 F1
Lenton Av *DERBYE* DE21 ....35 G5
Leominster Dr *DERBYE* DE21 .....36 B1
Leonard Cl *NORM/LIT* DE23 ....2 D7
Leonard St *NORM/LIT* DE23 ....2 D7
Leopold St *DERBY* DE1 ....2 D6
Leslie Cl *NORM/LIT* DE23...........50 B1
Leven Cl *DERBYSE* DE24 ....62 A2
Leveret Cl *MELB/CHEL* DE73.......64 A2
Lewis Cl *NORM/LIT* DE23 ....42 A5
Lewiston Rd *DERBYE* DE21 ....44 A1
Lexington Rd *DERBYE* DE21 ....44 A1
Leyland Gdns *DERBYW* DE22......33 H4
Leylands *DERBYW* * DE22...........33 H3
Leyland St *DERBYW* DE22..........33 H4
The Leys *DERBYE* DE21 ....19 H3
Leys Ct *BPR/DUF* * DE56 ....7 E3
Leys Field Gdns
       MELB/CHEL DE73..............63 H4
Leytonstone Dr *DERBYW* DE22 ...40 D1
Lichfield Dr *DERBYSE* DE24 ....53 H4

Lidgate Cl *MCKLVR* DE3 ....39 H5
Lilac Av *DERBYW* DE22 ....40 D1
Lilac Cl *DERBYSE* DE24 ....53 H3
Lilac Ct *DERBYSE* * DE24 ....53 H3
Lilley St *DERBYSE* DE24 ....54 A3
Lime Av *BPR/DUF* DE56 ....17 H1
       DERBY DE1 ....3 B7
       DERBYE DE21 ....35 E1
Lime Crs *DERBYSE* DE56 ....6 A4
Lime Cft *DERBYW* DE22 ....26 A4
Limedale Av *DERBYE* DE21 ....35 E1
Lime Gv *BWSH/BRSTN* DE72......56 C2
       DERBYE DE21 ....44 A1
Lime La *DERBYE* DE21 ....27 H5
Limerick Rd *DERBYE* DE21 ....44 A2
Limes Av *MCKLVR* DE3..............40 A5
Lime Wk *NORM/LIT* DE23 ....41 G5
Linacres Dr *MELB/CHEL* DE73 ....64 A2
Lincoln Av *DERBYSE* DE24 ....53 H1
Lincoln Gn *MELB/CHEL* DE73 .....63 G2
Lindale Wy *MELB/CHEL* DE73.....63 H2
Linden Cl *BPR/DUF* DE56 ....6 A4
Lindford Cl *DERBYE* DE21 ....27 G5
Lindisfarne Cl *DERBYSE* DE24 ....61 H2
Lindon Dr *DERBYSE* DE24 ....54 B3
Lindrick Cl *MCKLVR* DE3 ....39 H3
Lindsey Cl *DERBYE* DE21 ....35 F5
Lingfield Ri *MCKLVR* DE3 ....39 H3
Links Cl *DERBYE* DE21 ....52 A5
Linnet Cl *DERBYE* DE21.............37 E5
Linnet Hl *MCKLVR* DE3..............49 H2
Liskeard Dr *DERBYW* DE22 ....25 G4
Lismore Ct *DERBYE* DE21 ....61 G1
Liston Dr *DERBYW* DE22............34 A3
Litchurch La *DERBYSE* DE24.......2 E7
Litchurch St *NORM/LIT* DE23 ......2 E7
Little Bridge St *DERBY* DE1 ....2 A2
Littledale Cl *DERBYE* DE21 ....28 B5
Little Derby Hl
       RDERBYSW * DE65.............59 G1
Little Longstone Cl
       MCKLVR DE3 ....40 C4
Little Meadow Rd
       MELB/CHEL DE73..............63 H2
Littleover Crs *NORM/LIT* DE23 ....51 G1
Littleover La *NORM/LIT* DE23 .....51 G1
Little Woodbury Dr
       NORM/LIT DE23 ....50 C3
Litton Cl *BPR/DUF* DE56.............6 C2
Litton Dr *DERBYE* DE21 ....28 B5
Liverpool St *DERBY* DE21..........35 F3
Liversage Pl *DERBY* DE1 ....2 E6
Liversage St *DERBY* DE1 ....2 E6
Liversage St *DERBY* DE1 ....2 E5
Livingstone Rd
       NORM/LIT DE23 ....51 H5
Lochinvar Cl *DERBYE* DE21........45 E3
Lockington Cl *MELB/CHEL* DE73 ...63 G2
Lockington Rd *CDON/KEG* DE74...73 G2
Locko Rd *DERBYE* DE21 ....36 D4
Lockwood Rd *DERBYW* DE22.....25 G4
Locomotive Wy *DERBYSE* DE24 ...3 J7
Lodge Cl *BPR/DUF* DE56 ....17 H2
       RDERBYSW DE65...............48 B5
Lodge Dr *BPR/DUF* DE56 ....5 H2
Lodge La *ASHB* DE6 ....23 H4
       DERBY DE1 ....2 B2
       DERBYE DE21 ....44 D3
Lodge Ms *BWSH/BRSTN* * DE72 ...56 D2
Lodge St *BWSH/BRSTN* DE72 .....56 D2
Lodge Wy *MCKLVR* DE3.............40 A4
Lombard St *DERBYW* DE22........32 C5
Lomond Av *DERBYSE* DE24 ....62 A2
London Rd *BWSH/BRSTN* DE72...66 B2
       DERBY DE1 ....2 D5
       DERBYSE DE24 ....42 D3
Long Bridge La *DERBYSE* DE24 ...53 E1
Long Cft *BWSH/BRSTN* DE72 .....65 F4
Longford Cl *DERBYW* DE22 ....33 G1
Longford St *DERBYW* DE22 ....33 G1
Longlands La *RDERBYSW* DE65 ...59 H3
Longley La *DERBYE* DE21 ....36 C5
Longmoor La
       BWSH/BRSTN DE72............47 H5
Long Rw *BPR/DUF* DE56 ....5 H5
       BWSH/BRSTN DE72............67 E2
Longstock Cl *DERBYE* DE21 ....35 F2
Longstone Ri *BPR/DUF* DE56.......6 C1
Longstone Wk *DERBY* * DE1 ....2 B7
Longthorpe Cl *NORM/LIT* DE23 ...50 D2
Longwalls La *BPR/DUF* DE56.......5 F2
Lonsdale Pl *DERBYW* DE22.........41 G2
Loom Cl *BPR/DUF* DE56 ....6 D2
Lord St *DERBYSE* DE24 ....53 E3
Lorne St *DERBYW* DE22.............42 A4
Lorraine Cl *DERBYSE* DE24 ....63 F1
Loscoe-Denby La *RIPLEY* DE5 .....9 G3
Loscoe Gra *HEANOR* DE75 ....9 H4

Loscoe Rd *DERBYE* DE21 ....35 H2
Lothian Pl *CDON/KEG* DE74........72 D4
Lothlorien Cl *NORM/LIT* DE23 .....51 E2
Loudon St *DERBYSE* DE23 ....42 B3
Loudoun Pl *CDON/KEG* DE74......72 D3
Lousie Greaves La
       DERBYE DE21 ....36 D5
Louvain Rd *NORM/LIT* DE23 ....41 F3
Lower Dale Rd *NORM/LIT* DE23 ...42 A4
Lower Eley St *DERBY* DE1 ....2 B7
Lower Gn *RDERBYSW* DE65 ....60 A3
Lower Hall Cl *BPR/DUF* DE56 .....12 D4
Lower Rd *DERBYW* DE22 ....32 B3
Lowes La *MELB/CHEL* DE73 ....63 E3
Lowe St *DERBYSE* DE24 ....53 F2
Lowlands Rd *BPR/DUF* DE56 ....6 C3
Loxley Cl *DERBYE* DE21 ....36 A1
Loxton Ct *MCKLVR* DE3 ....39 H3
Loyne Cl *DERBYSE* DE24 ....62 A2
Luccombe Dr *DERBYSE* DE24.....54 C4
Lucerne Rd *DERBYE* DE21 ....28 B5
Ludgate Wk *DERBYW* DE22........40 B1
Ludlow Cl *DERBYE* DE21............45 E1
Lulworth Cl *NORM/LIT* DE23 ......51 G3
Lumb La *BPR/DUF* DE56 ....5 F5
Lundie Cl *DERBYSE* DE24 ....61 G2
Lupin Cl *DERBYE* DE21...............28 B5
Lychgate Cl *DERBYE* DE21 ....35 E1
Lydstep Cl *DERBYE* DE21 ....36 B1
Lyndhurst Gv *DERBYSE* DE21 .....43 H1
Lyndhurst St *NORM/LIT* DE23 .....42 B4
Lyndhurst Ter *NORM/LIT* * DE23 ...42 B3
Lynton St *DERBYW* DE22 ....41 H2
Lynwood Rd *DERBYSE* DE24 ......52 A5
Lytham Cl *DERBYE* DE21 ....35 E2
Lyttelton St *DERBYW* DE22........41 E1

M

Macaulay St *DERBYSE* DE24.......52 B4
Mackenzie St *DERBYW* DE22 .....33 F5
Macklin St *DERBY* DE1 ....2 B4
Mackworth Rd *DERBYW* DE22 ....33 H5
Macready Pl *DERBYSE* DE24 ......53 C2
Madeley Ct *MCKLVR* DE3...........40 A5
Madeley St *NORM/LIT* DE23 ......42 B4
Madison Av *DERBYE* DE21 ....35 F4
Maidstone Dr *DERBYSE* DE24 ....53 G4
Maidwell Cl *BPR/DUF* DE56 ....6 C2
Main Av *DERBYW* DE22 ....26 A3
Maine Dr *DERBYE* DE21.............35 H5
Main Rd *BWSH/BRSTN* DE72......55 F3
       ILK DE7 ....21 E3
Main St *BWSH/BRSTN* DE72 ......56 A3
       BWSH/BRSTN DE72............57 E2
       BWSH/BRSTN DE72............70 D3
       CDON/KEG DE74...............73 G3
       ILK DE7 ....14 A3
       MELB/CHEL DE73..............74 C5
       MELB/CHEL DE73..............76 B1
       MELB/CHEL DE73..............76 C3
       RDERBYSW DE65...............48 A5
       RDERBYSW DE65...............49 E4
       RDERBYSW DE65...............60 A3
Maize Cl *NORM/LIT* DE23 ....50 D3
Makeney Rd *BPR/DUF* DE56 ......12 B4
       BPR/DUF DE56 ....18 A3
Malcolm Gv *NORM/LIT* DE23 .....50 B2
Malcolm St *NORM/LIT* DE23 ......42 C4
Malham Rd *NORM/LIT* DE23 ......50 C3
Malin Cl *DERBYSE* DE24 ....54 A4
Mallard Wk *MCKLVR* DE3...........49 H2
Maltby Cl *DERBYW* DE22 ....34 A1
The Maltings
       BWSH/BRSTN DE72............66 D3
       DERBY * DE1 ....2 D6
Malton Pl *DERBYE* DE21 ....35 E2
Malvern Cl *MCKLVR* DE3 ....40 A3
Malvern Wy *DERBYE* DE21 ....35 E2
Manchester St *DERBYW* DE22 ....33 G5
Manifold Dr *DERBYSE* DE22 ....54 A1
Manor Av *DERBYW* DE22 ....41 F3
Manor Ct *BWSH/BRSTN* DE72.....57 G1
Manor Farm Rd
       BWSH/BRSTN DE72............65 G4
Manorleigh *BWSH/BRSTN* DE72 ...57 H1
Manor Pk *BWSH/BRSTN* DE72 ....45 F5
Manor Park Ct *DERBYW* * DE22...41 E3
Manor Park Wy *DERBYW* DE22 ...41 E3
Manor Rd *BPR/DUF* DE56 ....6 A4
       BWSH/BRSTN DE72............45 F5
       MELB/CHEL DE73..............63 G3
       NORM/LIT DE23................41 F4
Mansfield Rd *DERBY* DE1 ....2 D1

Mansfields Cft *RDERBYSW* DE65....48 A5
Mansfield St *DERBY* DE1............34 B4
Maple Av *NORM/LIT* DE23............51 G3
Maplebeck Ct *DERBY* DE1...........2 D1
Maple Dr *BPR/DUF* DE56............6 C5
  BWSH/BRSTN DE72...........65 F5
  DERBYSE DE24...............53 H3
  MELB/CHEL DE73............63 H2
Maple Gv *DERBYE* DE21............25 G3
Mapleton Av *DERBYE* DE21..........35 G2
Mapleton Rd *BWSH/BRSTN* DE72 ...56 C1
Marchington La *DERBYW* DE22......33 H2
Marcus St *DERBY* * DE1...........34 B4
Maree Cl *DERBYSE* DE24...........51 H5
Marfleet Cl *MCKLVR* DE3...........39 H3
Margaret Av *DERBYSE* DE24........43 F1
Margaret St *DERBY* DE1...........44 C1
Margreave Rd *DERBYE* DE21.........35 G4
Marigold Cl *DERBYE* DE21..........28 A5
Marina Dr *DERBYE* DE21...........44 C1
  DERBYSE DE24...............53 F4
Marina Rd *HEANOR* DE75...........15 G2
Marjorie Rd *DERBYSE* DE24........35 F3
Markeaton La *DERBYW* DE22........33 E3
Markeaton St *DERBY* DE1..........33 H5
Market Head *DERBY* DE56..........6 A4
Market Pl *BPR/DUF* DE56..........6 B4
  DERBY * DE1................2 C3
  MELB/CHEL DE73............76 A3
  RIPLEY DE5.................9 H1
Market St *BWSH/BRSTN* DE72......56 D2
  CDON/KEG DE74.............73 E4
Markham Ct *DERBYE* DE21.........35 G5
Mark's Cl *NORM/LIT* DE23.........51 G3
Marlborough Dr *BPR/DUF* DE56.....6 D2
Marlborough Rd
  BWSH/BRSTN DE72...........57 G2
  DERBYSE DE24...............52 C2
Marlowe Ct *NORM/LIT* DE23.......52 A3
Marsden Cl *BPR/DUF* DE56........17 H3
Marsden St *DERBYSE* DE24.........53 F2
Marshaw Cl *MCKLVR* DE3...........40 B5
Marshgreen Cl *DERBYSE* DE24.....54 C4
Marsh La *BPR/DUF* DE56...........6 C5
Marsh Lane Crs *BPR/DUF* DE56....6 C3
Marston Cl *BPR/DUF* DE56.........6 D1
  NORM/LIT DE23..............51 G4
Martindale Ct *BPR/DUF* DE56......7 E2
Martin Dr *DERBYE* DE21...........35 H3
Maryland Rd *DERBYE* DE21.........36 A5
Marylebone Crs *DERBYW* DE22......40 C1
Masefield Av *NORM/LIT* DE23......51 H2
Masson Wk *DERBYW* * DE22........41 H2
Matlock Houses *DERBYE* * DE21 ...44 D3
Matlock Rd *BPR/DUF* DE56.........6 A4
  DERBYSE DE24...............35 G2
Matthew St *DERBYSE* DE24........53 G3
Matthew Wy *NORM/LIT* DE23.......50 B2
Max Rd *DERBYE* DE21.............35 F3
Maxwell Av *DERBYW* DE22.........33 G3
Mayfair Crs *DERBYW* DE22........32 B5
Mayfield Av *BPR/DUF* DE56........13 H2
Mayfield Rd *DERBYE* DE21........35 F4
Maylands *BWSH/BRSTN* DE72......45 C5
Maylands Av
  BWSH/BRSTN DE72...........57 H1
Maypole La *NORM/LIT* DE23.......50 D3
May St *DERBYW* DE22.............2 A7
Maytree Cl *DERBYE* DE21.........28 B5
Mcneil Gv *BWSH/BRSTN* DE72......56 D2
Mead Cl *DERBYSE* DE24...........52 A5
Meadow Cl *BWSH/BRSTN* DE72 .....56 D1
  BWSH/BRSTN DE72...........57 H2
  DERBYE DE21...............44 D2
  ILK DE7...................14 C4
  RDERBYSW DE65.............60 A4
Meadow Ct *BPR/DUF* DE56.........6 A3
  BPR/DUF DE56..............13 H3
  BWSH/BRSTN DE72...........44 A3
Meadow Crs *CDON/KEG* DE74.......73 E5
Meadowgrass Cl
  NORM/LIT DE23..............51 E3
Meadow La *DERBY* DE1............3 F3
  DERBYSE DE24..............43 G1
  DERBYSE DE24..............43 G5
Meadowlark Gv *DERBYE* DE21 .....35 H2
Meadow Nook *DERBYSE* DE24 .....54 B5
Meadow Rd *DERBY* DE1............2 E1
Meadow V *BPR/DUF* DE56..........17 G2
Meadow View Cl *DERBYE* DE21 ....28 A5
Meadow Wy *MELB/CHEL* DE73......63 G3
Mear Dr *BWSH/BRSTN* DE72........45 G5
Meath Av *DERBYSE* DE24..........44 A2
Medina Cl *DERBYSE* DE24.........54 C4
Medway Dr *DERBYW* DE22.........26 B3
Meerbrook Cl *DERBYE* DE21.......35 H2
Megaloughton La *DERBYE* DE21....48 H3
Melbourn Cl *BPR/DUF* DE56.......17 H3

Melbourne Cl *BPR/DUF* DE56........6 B5
  DERBYW DE22...............33 G2
  MCKLVR DE3................40 C3
Melbourne Houses
  DERBY * DE1................44 D3
Melbourne La *MELB/CHEL* DE73 ...74 D5
Melbourne St *DERBY* DE1..........2 D7
Melbreak Cl *MCKLVR* DE3.........40 B5
Melfort Cl *DERBYSE* DE24........62 A2
Mellor's La *BPR/DUF* DE56........12 D4
Mellor St *DERBYSE* DE24.........53 F3
Melrose Cl *DERBYSE* DE24........61 H2
Melton Av *MELB/CHEL* DE73......75 H2
  NORM/LIT DE23.............51 F3
Melville Ct *RDERBYSW* DE65.......58 A1
Memorial Rd *DERBYW* DE22.......33 F1
Mendip Ct *DERBYE* DE21.........35 F1
Menin Rd *DERBYW* DE22..........33 F1
Mercaston La *DERBYW* DE22......23 H1
Mercaston Rd *DERBYE* DE21.......35 G3
Merchant Av *DERBYE* DE21........44 C2
Merchant St *DERBYW* DE22.......33 H5
Mercian Ms *DERBYE* DE21........44 C2
Mere Beck *BWSH/BRSTN* DE72 .....56 A3
Merion Gv *NORM/LIT* DE23.......40 D5
Merlin Cl *DERBYSE* DE24.........51 G5
Merlin Wy *MCKLVR* DE3...........49 H2
Merridale Rd *NORM/LIT* DE23 .....51 F2
Merrill Wy *DERBYSE* DE24........52 D4
Merrybower Cl *DERBYE* DE21......61 F1
Merthyr Ct *DERBYE* DE21........36 A1
Metcalfe Cl *DERBYSE* DE24.......54 A1
The Mews *MELB/CHEL* * DE73......76 A3
Meynell Ct *DERBYW* DE22........33 F1
Meynell St *NORM/LIT* DE23.......42 A4
Michelle Cl *DERBYSE* DE24.......61 F1
Michigan Cl *DERBYE* DE21.......44 B1
Micklecroft Gdns
  NORM/LIT DE23.............50 B2
Mickleross Cl *MCKLVR* DE3.......40 A2
Middlebeck Cl *MELB/CHEL* DE73 ...63 G3
Middleton Av *NORM/LIT* DE23 .....41 F1
  RIPLEY DE5................9 G2
Middleton Dr *NORM/LIT* DE23 .....41 F1
Midland Pl *DERBY* DE1...........3 G6
Midland Rd *DERBY* DE1..........3 F7
Midshires Wy *BPR/DUF* DE56......5 F1
  ILK DE7...................29 E2
Midway *DERBYW* DE22...........33 H1
Milbank Cl *DERBYW* DE22........32 B5
Milburn Gdns *DERBYE* DE21.......28 A5
Milbury Ct *DERBY* DE1..........35 G1
Mile Ash La *DERBYW* DE22.......34 A2
Milford Rd *BPR/DUF* DE56........17 H1
Milford St *DERBY* DE1..........34 A4
Millbank Av *BPR/DUF* DE56.......6 C5
Mill Cl *BPR/DUF* DE56..........13 H3
  BWSH/BRSTN DE72...........45 H5
  RDERBYSW DE65............60 A2
Mill Cft *MCKLVR* DE3...........40 A2
Milldale Cl *RIPLEY* DE5.........8 C1
Milldale Ct *BPR/DUF* DE56.......6 C4
Milldale Rd *DERBYE* DE21.......45 E3
Millennium Wy *DERBYSE* DE24 ....43 F2
Millersdale Av *BPR/DUF* DE56.....6 C2
Millfield *BWSH/BRSTN* DE72......67 G2
Mill Gn *BWSH/BRSTN* * DE72......66 D3
Mill Hi La *BWSH/BRSTN* DE72 .....47 H5
  NORM/LIT DE23.............42 A3
Mill Hill Rd *NORM/LIT* DE23 .....42 A3
Millhouse Ct *BWSH/BRSTN* DE72...57 G2
Mill La *BPR/DUF* DE56...........6 C3
  MCKLVR DE3...............40 A2
Mill Meadow Wy
  RDERBYSW DE65............48 A5
Mill Moor Cl *MELB/CHEL* DE73 ....63 F2
Millom Pl *DERBYE* DE21........35 G2
Mill Rw *DERBY* * DE21.........44 C1
Mills Cl *BWSH/BRSTN* DE72......56 D2
Mill St *BPR/DUF* DE56..........6 A3
  DERBY DE1................33 H5
Milner Av *BWSH/BRSTN* DE72 .....56 D2
Milton Cl *MCKLVR* DE3..........39 H3
Milton St *DERBYW* DE22........41 G2
Milward Rd *HEANOR* DE75.........9 H5
Mimosa Crs *NORM/LIT* DE23......51 H4
Minster Rd *DERBYE* DE21........35 F1
Minton Rd *CDON/KEG* DE74.......72 D3
Misterton Cl *DERBYE* DE21......33 H1
The Moat *CDON/KEG* DE74........73 H4
Moira Cl *DERBYE* DE21.........35 H4
Moira Dl *CDON/KEG* DE74........73 H4
Moira St *MELB/CHEL* DE73.......75 H3
Molineux St *NORM/LIT* DE23......42 C4
Monarch Dr *DERBYE* DE21........28 C5
Moncrieff Crs *DERBYE* DE21......35 H3
Mondello Dr *DERBYSE* DE24......54 B3

Monks Cl *DERBYSE* DE24..........61 F2
Monk St *DERBYW* DE22...........2 A5
Monmouth St *DERBYE* DE21.......3 J1
Monsal Dr *DERBYE* DE21.........45 E3
Monteith Cl *CDON/KEG* DE74......73 E4
Montford Ms *CDON/KEG* DE74.....73 E3
Montpelier *DERBYW* DE22........25 C1
Montrose Cl *DERBYSE* DE24.......51 H5
Monyash Cl *DERBYE* DE21........35 H3
Monyash Wy *BPR/DUF* DE56.......6 C2
Moor Dr *DERBYSE* DE24.........53 H4
Moor End *DERBYE* DE21.........44 D1
Moore St *NORM/LIT* DE23........42 B3
Moorfield Rd *BPR/DUF* DE56......12 D3
Moorgate *DERBYW* DE22..........32 B5
Moorhead Av *DERBYSE* DE24.......53 G4
Moorland Rd *MCKLVR* DE3........40 A3
Moor La *ASHB* DE6..............31 E1
  BWSH/BRSTN DE72...........37 H4
  BWSH/BRSTN DE72...........65 G4
  DERBYE DE21...............19 E4
  DERBYSE DE24..............52 D3
  DERBYSE DE24..............62 D3
Moorpool Crs *BPR/DUF* DE56......12 D2
Moor Ri *BPR/DUF* DE56..........12 D2
Moorside Crs *DERBYSE* DE24......52 A5
Moorside La *BPR/DUF* DE56......12 D2
Moor St *DERBYSE* DE24.........44 D1
Moorway Cft *NORM/LIT* DE23 .....51 E2
Moorway La *NORM/LIT* DE23......50 D4
Moray Wk *DERBY* * DE1.........34 D3
Morefern Dr *DERBYE* DE21.......35 C3
Morledge *DERBY* DE1...........2 D4
Morleston St *NORM/LIT* DE23 .....42 C3
Morley Almshouses La *ILK* DE7 ...28 A1
Morley Cl *BPR/DUF* DE56........7 F1
Morley Gdns *DERBYE* DE21.......36 A3
Morley La *ILK* DE7............19 G5
  ILK DE7..................29 G2
Morley Rd *DERBYE* DE21........35 H4
Morley St *DERBYW* DE22........33 G5
Morlich Dr *DERBYSE* DE24.......51 H5
Morningside Cl *DERBYSE* DE24 ....53 E5
Mornington Crs *DERBYW* DE22 ....33 E5
Morpeth Gdns *DERBYE* DE21......35 E1
Morrell Wood Dr *BPR/DUF* DE56...7 F2
Mortimer St *DERBYSE* DE24......52 C2
Moscow Cottages
  BPR/DUF * DE56............12 A5
Mosedale Cl *DERBYSE* DE24.......53 C1
Moses La *ILK* DE7.............28 D1
Moss St *DERBYW* DE22..........41 H3
Mossvale Dr *NORM/LIT* DE23......50 D3
Mostyn Av *NORM/LIT* DE23.......41 G5
Mottistone Cl *DERBYSE* DE24 .....54 C4
Moult Av *DERBYE* DE21.........44 D2
Moulton Cl *BPR/DUF* DE56........7 E2
Mountbatten Cl *DERBYSE* DE24 ...53 F5
Mount Carmel St
  NORM/LIT DE23.............42 A3
Mountfield Wy *DERBYSE* DE24 ....54 C5
Mountford Cl *DERBYE* DE21......36 A1
Mount Pleasant *CDON/KEG* DE74...73 E4
Mount Pleasant Dr
  BPR/DUF DE56.............5 H2
Mount St *DERBY* DE1..........2 C7
Mowbray Gdns *DERBYSE* DE24 ....52 D2
Mowbray St *DERBYSE* DE24......52 D1
Moy Av *DERBYSE* DE24.........52 D3
Moyne Gdns *MELB/CHEL* DE73 ....63 H4
Muirfield Dr *MCKLVR* DE3.......40 C5
Mulberries Ct *DERBYW* DE22 .....25 H4
Mulberry Cl *BPR/DUF* DE56.......6 C4
Mulberry Ms *RIPLEY* DE5........8 B1
Mulberry Wy
  BWSH/BRSTN DE72...........71 F1
Mull Ct *DERBYSE* DE24.........61 G1
Mullion Pl *DERBYSE* DE24.......54 A4
Mundy Cl *DERBY* DE1..........33 H5
Mundy St *DERBY* DE1..........33 H5
Murray Rd *MCKLVR* DE3........40 C2
Murray St *DERBYSE* DE24.......53 C1
Muswell Rd *DERBYW* DE22.......40 B1
Myers Cl *DERBYSE* DE24........52 A5

N

Nailers Wy *BPR/DUF* DE56........6 D2
Nairn Av *DERBYE* DE21..........35 E4
Nairn Cl *DERBYSE* DE24.........61 G1
Namur Cl *DERBYW* DE22.........41 F3
Napier Cl *MCKLVR* DE3.........40 A2
Napier St *DERBYW* DE22........41 F1
Naseby Cl *MCKLVR* DE3.........39 G3

Naseby Rd *BPR/DUF* DE56 7
Nearwood Dr *DERBYE* DE21 27
Neilson St *DERBYSE* DE24 53
Nelson Cl *MCKLVR* DE3 40
Nelson St *DERBY* DE1 3
Nesfield Cl *DERBYSE* DE24 54
Ness Wk *DERBYW* DE22 25
Nether Cl *BPR/DUF* DE56 11
Netherclose St *NORM/LIT* DE23 42
Netherfield La *CDON/KEG* DE74 ...67
Nether La *BPR/DUF* DE56 10
  BPR/DUF DE56 13
Netherside Dr *MELB/CHEL* DE73 ...63
Netherwood Ct *DERBYW* DE22 25
Nettlefold Crs *MELB/CHEL* DE73...76
Nevinson Av *NORM/LIT* DE23 51
Nevinson Dr *NORM/LIT* DE23 51
Nevis Cl *DERBYSE* DE24 61
Newark Rd *DERBYE* DE21 35
Newbold Av *DERBYSE* DE24 53
Newbold Cl *MELB/CHEL* DE73 63
Newbold Dr *CDON/KEG* DE74 73
Newborough Rd *DERBYSE* DE24....54
New Breck Rd *BPR/DUF* DE56 6
Newbridge Crs *DERBYSE* DE24 53
Newbury St *DERBYSE* DE24 53
Newdigate St *ILK* DE7 21
  NORM/LIT DE23 52
Newgate Cl *MELB/CHEL* DE73 64
Newhaven Rd *DERBYE* DE21 36
New Inn La *DERBYE* DE21 26
Newland St *DERBY* DE1 2
Newlyn Dr *NORM/LIT* DE23 52
Newmarket Ct *DERBYSE* DE24 53
Newmarket Dr *DERBYSE* DE24 53
New Mount Cl *NORM/LIT* DE23 51
Newport Cl *DERBYSE* DE24 54
Newquay Pl *DERBYSE* DE24 54
New Rd *BPR/DUF* DE56 6
  DERBYW DE22 34
Newstead Av *DERBYE* DE21 35
New St *BWSH/BRSTN* DE72 45
  BWSH/BRSTN DE72 56
  DERBY DE1 3
  DERBYE DE21 18
Newton's Wk *DERBYW* DE22 33
New Zealand La *BPR/DUF* DE56 ...17
New Zealand Sq *DERBYW* DE22 ...41
Nicholas Cl *DERBYSE* DE24 36
Nicola Gdns *NORM/LIT* DE23 51
Nightingale Rd *DERBYSE* DE24 52
Noel St *DERBYW* * DE22 33
The Nook *BPR/DUF* * DE56 12
  HEANOR DE75 9
  MELB/CHEL DE73 68
Nooning La *BWSH/BRSTN* DE72....56
Norbury Cl *DERBYW* DE22 33
Norbury Ct *DERBYW* * DE22 33
Norbury Crs *NORM/LIT* DE23 51
Norbury Wy *BPR/DUF* DE56 6
Norfolk Gdns *DERBYW* * DE22 34
Norfolk St *NORM/LIT* DE23 42
Norman Av *NORM/LIT* DE23 51
Normanton La *NORM/LIT* DE23 41
Normanton Rd *DERBY* DE1 2
  NORM/LIT DE23 42
Northacre Rd *DERBYE* DE21 36
North Av *DERBYW* DE22 26
  MCKLVR DE3 40
North Cl *MCKLVR* DE3 40
Northfield *BPR/DUF* DE56 7
  DERBYSE DE24 61
North La *BPR/DUF* DE56 5
Northmead Dr *DERBYW* DE22 41
North Pde *DERBY* DE1 34
North Rw *DERBYW* DE22 33
North St *DERBY* DE1 34
  MELB/CHEL DE73 75
  NORM/LIT DE23 41
North Ter *BPR/DUF* * DE56 6
Northumberland St
  NORM/LIT DE23 42
Northway Dr *DERBY* * DE1 41
Northwood Av *DERBYE* DE21 35
Norwich St *DERBYSE* DE24 35
Norwood Cl *DERBYW* DE22 40
Nottingham Rd *BPR/DUF* DE56 6
  DERBY DE1 3
  DERBYE DE21 35
  DERBYE DE21 45
Nunsfield Dr *DERBYSE* DE24 54
Nun's St *DERBY* DE1 33
Nursery Cl *BWSH/BRSTN* DE72....45
Nutwood Cl *DERBYW* DE22 26

O

Oadby Ri NORM/LIT DE23 51 H3
Oak Cl BPR/DUF DE56 17 H3
BWSH/BRSTN DE72 45 H1
DERBYW DE22 25 H4
Oak Crs NORM/LIT DE23 51 F1
Oakdale Gdns DERBYE DE21 28 A5
Oak Dr DERBYSE DE24 53 H3
MCKLVR DE3 40 B3
Oakfield Ct ILK DE7 21 F4
Oakham Cl DERBYE DE21 35 E2
Oakhurst Cl BPR/DUF DE56 5 G1
Oaklands Av NORM/LIT DE23 51 F4
Oaklands Cl RIPLEY DE5 14 B1
Oaklands Rd RDERBYSW DE65 48 B5
Oaklands Wy MELB/CHEL DE73 76 A2
Oakleigh Av DERBYE DE21 35 G5
Oakover Dr DERBYW DE22 25 G5
Oakridge DERBYE DE21 36 A4
Oak Rd BWSH/BRSTN DE72 55 E5
The Oaks DERBYE DE21 18 D5
Oakside Wy DERBYE DE21 28 A5
Oak St NORM/LIT DE23 42 B4
Oaktree Av DERBYSE DE24 52 C2
Oak Tree Ct BWSH/BRSTN DE72 45 H5
Oakwood Cl DERBYSE DE24 61 G2
Oakwood Dr DERBYE DE21 36 A1
Offerton Av NORM/LIT DE23 51 H1
Old Barn Cl DERBYE * DE21 18 D5
Old Blacksmiths Yd DERBY * DE1 2 C3
Oldbury Cl DERBYE DE21 35 G1
Old Chester Rd DERBY DE1 34 B3
Old Church Cl DERBYW DE22 25 F3
Old Gate Av BWSH/BRSTN DE72 70 D2
Old Hall Av BPR/DUF DE56 17 G2
DERBYSE DE24 54 A2
NORM/LIT DE23 41 E5
Old Hall Rd NORM/LIT DE23 41 F5
Old La DERBYW DE22 34 B1
Old Mansfield Rd DERBYE DE21 34 D2
Old Mill Cl BPR/DUF DE56 17 H2
Old Pit La ILK DE7 15 F4
Old Station Cl RDERBYSW DE65 58 A1
Old Vicarage Cl NORM/LIT DE23 41 F5
Old Vicarage La DERBYW DE22 25 F3
Olive St DERBYW DE22 41 H2
Olivier St NORM/LIT DE23 42 C5
Olton Rd MCKLVR DE3 39 H2
Onslow Rd MCKLVR DE3 40 A2
Opal Cl DERBYE DE21 35 H1
Openwoodgate BPR/DUF DE56 6 D3
Openwood Rd BPR/DUF DE56 7 E4
The Orchard BPR/DUF DE56 6 B3
Orchard Av CDON/KEG DE74 72 D4
Orchard Cl BPR/DUF DE56 12 C2
BWSH/BRSTN DE72 45 H2
BWSH/BRSTN DE72 57 H1
DERBYSE DE24 54 B5
ILK DE7 27 E4
MELB/CHEL DE73 75 H3
NORM/LIT DE23 51 F2
Orchard Cottages
BPR/DUF * DE56 6 B3
Orchard Ct DERBYE DE21 44 D1
The Orchards DERBYW DE22 25 G5
Orchard St DERBY DE1 2 B2
MCKLVR DE3 40 A5
ILK DE7 14 C4
Orchard Wy MELB/CHEL DE73 63 G2
Ordish Av DERBYE DE21 43 G1
Oregon Wy DERBYE DE21 44 B1
Oriel Ct DERBY * DE1 42 C3
Orkney Cl DERBYSE DE24 61 G1
Orly Av CDON/KEG DE74 72 D5
Ormskirk Ri DERBYE DE21 45 E2
Orton Wy BPR/DUF DE56 6 C1
Osmaston Park Rd
DERBYSE DE24 52 D2
Osmaston Rd DERBY DE1 2 D5
Osnabruck Sq DERBY * DE1 2 D4
Osprey Cl DERBYSE DE24 61 H2
Osterly Gn DERBYW DE22 40 D1
Oswestry Cl DERBYE DE21 28 A5
Otterburn Dr DERBYW DE22 33 F1
Otter St DERBY DE1 34 B4
Oulton Cl DERBYSE DE24 53 E5
Outram Wy DERBYSE DE24 61 H2
Oval Ct NORM/LIT DE23 51 F1
Overdale Rd NORM/LIT DE23 41 H4
Over La BPR/DUF DE56 4 D5
BPR/DUF DE56 7 F2
Overstone Cl BPR/DUF DE56 7 E3
Owlers La DERBYW DE22 41 F4
Owlswick Cl NORM/LIT DE23 50 D1
Oxenhope Cl NORM/LIT DE23 50 B2
Oxford St DERBY DE1 3 F7
DERBYE DE21 44 D1

P

Pack Horse Rd MELB/CHEL DE73 76 A1
The Paddock BPR/DUF DE56 12 D4
BWSH/BRSTN DE72 45 H2
DERBYSE DE24 54 C5
Paddock Cl CDON/KEG DE74 72 C4
Paddock Cft DERBYE DE21 35 G1
Padley Cl DERBYW DE22 26 B3
Padstow Cl DERBYSE DE24 61 G1
Padstow Rd DERBYSE DE24 54 B4
Palatine Gv NORM/LIT DE23 50 C2
Palladium Dr NORM/LIT DE23 50 D3
Pall Ml ILK DE7 27 F4
Palm Cl NORM/LIT DE23 40 D5
Palmerston Ct
MELB/CHEL DE73 76 A3
Palmerston St NORM/LIT DE23 41 H5
The Parade MCKLVR * DE3 40 A5
Parcel Ter DERBYW DE22 41 G1
Pares Wy BWSH/BRSTN DE72 45 H1
Pargate Cl RIPLEY DE5 8 C1
Park Av CDON/KEG DE74 72 C4
ILK DE7 29 H2
Park Cl BPR/DUF DE56 13 H2
DERBYE DE21 18 C5
Park Dr NORM/LIT DE23 41 F5
Parker Cl DERBY DE1 2 A1
Parker St DERBY DE1 34 A4
Park Farm Dr DERBYW DE22 33 G1
Parkfields Dr DERBYW DE22 33 H3
Park Gv DERBYW DE22 33 H3
Park Hall Rd RIPLEY DE5 7 H4
Park Hill Dr NORM/LIT DE23 52 A2
Park Homes DERBYSE * DE24 63 E1
Parklands Dr MELB/CHEL DE73 63 H4
Park La BWSH/BRSTN DE72 70 D3
CDON/KEG DE74 72 A4
DERBYW DE22 26 A4
NORM/LIT DE23 41 F5
Park Leys Ct DERBYE DE21 44 D2
Park Rd BPR/DUF DE56 6 B5
BPR/DUF DE56 17 H2
DERBYE DE21 44 C1
MCKLVR DE3 40 A4
Park Side BPR/DUF DE56 6 B4
Parkside Rd DERBYE DE21 43 H1
Parkstone Ct MCKLVR DE3 39 H4
Park St DERBY DE1 3 F6
Park Vw BWSH/BRSTN DE72 65 G5
DERBYE DE21 18 D5
Park View Cl DERBYW DE22 26 A4
Parkway MELB/CHEL DE73 63 G3
Park Wy RDERBYSW DE65 48 B4
Parliament Cl DERBYW DE22 41 H2
Parliament St DERBYW DE22 41 H2
Parliament Street Mills
DERBYW * DE22 41 H2
Parsons Gv RIPLEY DE5 8 C5
Partridge Wy MCKLVR DE3 40 D3
The Pastures BPR/DUF DE56 17 H1
Pastures Av NORM/LIT DE23 50 C2
Pastures Hl NORM/LIT DE23 50 D1
Paterson Av DERBYE DE21 35 H5
Patmore Sq NORM/LIT DE23 52 A3
Pattern Yd BPR/DUF * DE56 6 B4
Pavilion Rd NORM/LIT DE23 51 F1
Paxton Cl MCKLVR DE3 39 H5
Payne St DERBYW * DE22 33 G5
Peach St DERBYW DE22 41 G1
Peakdale Cl RIPLEY DE5 8 C1
Peak Dr DERBYSE DE24 52 B2
Pearl Cl DERBYE DE21 35 H1
Peartree Cl CDON/KEG DE74 72 D4
Pear Tree Crs NORM/LIT DE23 52 B1
Pear Tree Rd NORM/LIT DE23 42 B5
Pear Tree St NORM/LIT DE23 52 B1
Peatburn Av HEANOR DE75 9 H5
Peckham Gdns DERBYW DE22 40 D1
Peebles Cl DERBYSE DE24 61 H2
Peel St DERBYW DE22 33 G5
Peers Cl DERBYE DE21 36 A1
Peet St DERBYW DE22 41 H2
Pegwell Cl NORM/LIT DE23 51 G2
Pelham St DERBYW DE22 2 A6
Pembroke St DERBYE DE21 35 E3
Penalton Cl DERBYSE DE24 53 F3
Pendennis Cl DERBYSE DE24 54 A3
Pendlebury Dr MCKLVR DE3 40 B5
Pendleside Wy NORM/LIT DE23 50 B2
Penge Rd DERBYW DE22 32 D4
Penhaligan's Cl
MELB/CHEL DE73 63 G3
Peniston Ri MELB/CHEL DE73 75 H4
Penn La MELB/CHEL DE73 75 H3
Penn St BPR/DUF DE56 6 B3
Pennycress Cl NORM/LIT DE23 50 D2
Penny Long La DERBYW DE22 33 H3
Penrhyn Av NORM/LIT DE23 51 G1
Penrith Pl DERBYE DE21 35 E1
Pentewen Cl DERBYW DE22 33 H1
Pentland Cl DERBYE DE21 35 H1
Penzance Rd DERBYSE DE24 54 A4
Percy St DERBYW DE22 41 H3
Peregrine Cl DERBYSE DE24 51 G5
Perth Cl MCKLVR DE3 40 B2
Perth St DERBYE DE21 35 E2
Peterborough St
DERBYE DE21 35 F3
Peterhouse Ter
NORM/LIT * DE23 42 C4
Peterlee Pl DERBYSE DE24 53 H3
Petersham Dr DERBYSE DE24 54 B3
Petty Close La ASHB DE6 30 B2
Peveril Av BWSH/BRSTN DE72 45 H4
Peveril St DERBYSE DE24 53 E3
Pheasant Field Dr
DERBYE DE21 37 F5
Philips Cft BPR/DUF DE56 17 H1
Phoenix St DERBY DE1 2 D2
Pickering Ri DERBYE DE21 34 D2
Pilgrims Wy DERBYSE DE24 61 F2
Pilsley Cl BPR/DUF DE56 6 D1
Pimlico DERBYW DE22 33 E5
Pimm's Rd ASHB DE6 31 F3
Pinchom's Hill Rd
BPR/DUF DE56 6 C4
Pine Cl DERBYE DE21 44 A2
ILK DE7 15 E5
RDERBYSW DE65 48 A5
Pinecroft Ct DERBYE DE21 36 A2
The Pines BWSH/BRSTN DE72 57 E2
Pinewood Rd BPR/DUF DE56 5 H1
The Pinfold BPR/DUF DE56 6 D2
BWSH/BRSTN DE72 55 E5
The Pingle DERBYE DE21 44 D2
Pingle DERBYW DE22 25 H4
Pingle Crs BPR/DUF DE56 6 A2
Pinglehill Wy MELB/CHEL DE73 64 A2
Pingle La BPR/DUF DE56 6 A2
Pingreaves Dr
MELB/CHEL DE73 63 H2
Pippin Hl RIPLEY DE5 14 D1
Pit Close La MELB/CHEL DE73 63 H3
Pittar St DERBYW DE22 2 A7
Plackett Cl BWSH/BRSTN DE72 57 G1
Plains La BPR/DUF DE56 5 E3
Plantain Gdns NORM/LIT DE23 51 F4
Platts Av HEANOR DE75 15 H1
Plimsoll St DERBYW DE22 33 F5
Ploughfield Cl NORM/LIT DE23 51 E3
Plough Ga DERBYW DE22 34 A1
Pole's Rd ASHB DE6 31 F3
Pollards Oaks
BWSH/BRSTN DE72 45 G5
Pond Rd BPR/DUF DE56 12 D3
Ponsonby Ter DERBY DE1 41 H1
Pontefract St DERBYSE DE24 53 E2
Pontypool Cl DERBYE DE21 36 A1
Pool Cl DERBYSE DE24 54 B5
Poole St DERBYSE DE24 53 F3
Pool Rd MELB/CHEL DE73 76 B4
Poplar Av DERBYE DE21 44 D1
Poplar Cl DERBYSE DE24 54 A2
Poplar Nook DERBYW DE22 26 A4
Poplar Rw DERBYW DE22 34 B2
Porter Rd NORM/LIT DE23 41 H4
Porter's La DERBYE DE21 27 G5
RDERBYSW DE65 60 A2
Porthcawl Pl DERBYE DE21 36 B1
Portico Rd NORM/LIT DE23 50 D3
Portland Cl MCKLVR DE3 40 A4
Portland St NORM/LIT DE23 52 B1
RDERBYSW DE65 48 A5
Portman Cha DERBYSE DE24 61 G2
Portreath Dr DERBYW DE22 25 H5
Port Wy DERBYE DE21 19 E1
Portway Cl DERBYW DE22 26 B4
Posy La BWSH/BRSTN DE72 65 F5
Potter St DERBYE DE21 44 C2
MELB/CHEL DE73 76 A3
Pottery Cl BPR/DUF DE56 6 D2
Pottery La RIPLEY DE5 8 B4
Powell St NORM/LIT DE23 41 H4
Poynter Cl HEANOR DE75 15 H1
Poyser Av DERBYE DE21 35 H4
Poyser La ASHB DE6 31 F2
Prescot Cl MCKLVR DE3 39 H5
Prestbury Cl DERBYE DE21 36 A2
Priestland Av DERBYE DE21 44 C2
Primary Cl BPR/DUF DE56 6 B3
Prime Pkwy DERBY DE1 2 E1
Primrose Cl DERBYE DE21 27 G5
Primrose Dr ILK DE7 20 B5
Primula Wy NORM/LIT DE23 51 G5
Prince Charles Av
DERBYW DE22 40 C1
Princes Dr NORM/LIT DE23 41 E4
Princess Cl HEANOR DE75 15 H1
Princess Dr BWSH/BRSTN DE72 45 F5
Princes St NORM/LIT DE23 42 B5
Priors Barn Cl
BWSH/BRSTN DE72 45 H4
Priorway Av BWSH/BRSTN DE72 45 H4
Priorway Gdns
BWSH/BRSTN DE72 45 H5
Priory Cl MELB/CHEL DE73 63 H3
Priory Gdns DERBYE DE21 27 G5
Pritchett Dr NORM/LIT DE23 50 B1
Prospect Dr BPR/DUF DE56 6 A5
Prospect Rd RIPLEY DE5 13 H1
Provident St NORM/LIT DE23 42 A4
Pulborough Gdns
NORM/LIT DE23 50 C3
Pullman Rd DERBYE DE21 43 G2
Purchase Av HEANOR DE75 9 H5
Putney Cl DERBYW DE22 40 B1
Pybus St DERBYW DE22 33 G5
Pykestone Cl DERBYE DE21 35 G1
Pytchley Cl BPR/DUF DE56 7 E3

Q

Quantock Cl DERBYSE DE24 61 G2
Quarndon Hts DERBYW DE22 33 F1
Quarndon Vw DERBYW DE22 33 F1
Quarn Dr DERBYW DE22 25 F5
Quarn Gdns DERBY * DE1 34 A4
Quarn St DERBY DE1 33 H5
Quarn Wy DERBY DE1 2 A1
Quarry Rd BPR/DUF DE56 6 A5
ILK DE7 20 A4
Queen Mary Ct DERBYW DE22 34 A4
Queens Av ILK DE7 29 H2
Queensbury Cha
NORM/LIT DE23 50 D2
Queens Ct BWSH/BRSTN * DE72 56 D2
DERBYW * DE22 33 H3
Queen's Dr BPR/DUF DE56 5 H2
NORM/LIT DE23 41 F4
Queensferry Gdns
DERBYSE DE24 53 E5
Queensgate Dr
MELB/CHEL DE73 63 F4
Queensland Cl MCKLVR DE3 40 B2
Queen St BPR/DUF DE56 6 B4
DERBY DE1 2 C2
Queensway CDON/KEG DE74 72 C3
DERBYW DE22 33 G4
MELB/CHEL DE73 76 A2
Quick Cl MELB/CHEL DE73 75 H3
Quick Hill Rd DERBYSE DE24 61 F2
Quillings Wy BWSH/BRSTN DE72 46 A5
Quorn Ri NORM/LIT DE23 51 H3

R

Rabown Av NORM/LIT DE23 51 G1
Radbourne Ga MCKLVR DE3 40 A1
Radbourne La ASHB DE6 39 H1
DERBYW DE22 32 C4
Radbourne St DERBYW DE22 33 F5
Radcliffe Av DERBYE DE21 35 G4
Radcliffe Dr DERBYW DE22 41 G3
Radford Rd ILK DE7 15 E4
Radford St DERBYSE DE24 53 G2
Radnor St DERBYE DE21 35 E4
Radstock Gdns DERBYE DE21 35 F1
Radstone Cl DERBYE DE21 36 A1
Raglan Av DERBYW DE22 41 F1
Railway Ter DERBY DE1 3 G6
Rainham Gdns DERBYSE DE24 53 H4
Rainier Dr DERBYE DE21 35 H5
Raleigh St DERBYW DE22 41 F1
Ramblers Dr DERBYE DE21 28 B5
Ramsdean Cl DERBYE DE21 35 E3
Ramshaw Wy DERBYW * DE22 41 H2
Randolph Rd NORM/LIT DE23 52 A1
Ranelagh Gdns DERBYW DE22 33 E4
Rangemore Cl MCKLVR DE3 40 B2
Rannoch Cl DERBYE DE21 45 E1
DERBYW DE22 25 H5
Ranworth Cl DERBYSE DE24 63 E1
Raven Oak Cl BPR/DUF DE56 6 B5
Ravenscourt Rd DERBYW DE22 33 E5

Ravenscroft Dr *DERBYE* DE21............35 C5
Ravensdale Rd *DERBYE* DE22.........25 F5
Raven St *DERBYW* DE22............41 H3
Rawdon Cl *CDON/KEG* DE74.........72 D3
Rawdon St *NORM/LIT* DE23.........42 A4
Rawlinson Av *NORM/LIT* DE23........52 B2
Rawson Gn *BPR/DUF* DE56........13 G1
Raynesway *DERBYE* DE21............44 A3
  DERBYSE DE24.........................53 H2
Raynesway Park Dr
  DERBYE DE21.........................43 H5
Reader St *DERBYE* DE21.........44 D1
Rectory Gdns
  BWSH/BRSTN DE72.................65 F5
Rectory La *ILK* DE7............27 E4
Rectory Ms
  BWSH/BRSTN DE72.................65 F5
Rectory Rd *BWSH/BRSTN* DE72...57 H1
Reculver Cl *NORM/LIT* DE23........51 C2
Redbury Cl *DERBY* DE1............41 H2
Redcar Gdns *DERBYE* DE21.........35 E2
Redhill Ct *BPR/DUF* DE56............6 C5
Redland Cl *DERBYE* DE24........52 A5
Red La *BPR/DUF* DE56.............12 C4
Redmires Dr *MELB/CHEL* DE73....63 H2
Redruth Pl *DERBYE* DE24........54 B4
Redshaw St *DERBYW* DE22........33 H4
Redstart Cl *DERBYE* DE21........37 E5
Redway Cft *MELB/CHEL* DE73....75 C4
Redwing Cft *NORM/LIT* DE23........51 G2
Redwood Dr *DERBYSE* DE24.........61 H1
Reeves Rd *NORM/LIT* DE23........42 C5
Regal Ga *MELB/CHEL* DE73.........63 G4
Regency Cl *NORM/LIT* DE23........52 C4
Regent St *DERBY* DE1............3 F7
Reginald Rd North
  DERBYE DE21.........................35 G4
Reginald Rd South
  DERBYE DE21.........................35 G5
Reginald St *NORM/LIT* DE23.........42 C4
Regis Cl *DERBYE* DE21........36 A1
Reigate Dr *DERBYW* DE22.........32 C4
Renals St *NORM/LIT* DE23.........42 B3
Renfrew St *DERBYE* DE21........35 F4
Repton Av *NORM/LIT* DE23........51 H1
Retford Cl *DERBYE* DE21........35 E1
Ribblesdale Cl *DERBYW* DE22......33 F1
Richardson Dr *ILK* DE7........15 E4
Richardson St *DERBYW* DE22....33 G5
Richmond Av *NORM/LIT* DE23......51 F1
Richmond Cl *NORM/LIT* DE23......50 D2
Richmond Dr *BPR/DUF* DE56......11 G5
Richmond Rd *DERBYE* DE21........35 G5
  NORM/LIT DE23......................42 B5
Riddings *DERBYW* DE22........25 H4
Riddings La *ASHB* DE6........30 A1
Riddings St *DERBYW* DE22........2 A7
Ridgeway *MELB/CHEL* DE73........63 H4
Ridgeway Av *NORM/LIT* DE23......51 F3
Ridgewood Ct *DERBYE* DE21........35 F1
Riding Bank *MELB/CHEL* DE73....75 H5
The Ridings *BWSH/BRSTN* DE72 ...37 H5
Rigga La *BPR/DUF* DE56........18 B4
Rigsby Ct *MCKLVR* DE3........39 H3
Rimsdale Cl *DERBYSE* DE24........61 H1
Ripley Houses *DERBYE* DE21.......44 D3
Ripon Crs *DERBYE* DE21........35 F3
The Rise *DERBYW* DE22........33 H1
Risley La *BWSH/BRSTN* DE72........47 G4
Rivenhall Cl *NORM/LIT* DE23........50 C2
Riverside Ct *DERBYE* DE24........3 K6
Riverside Rd *DERBYSE* DE24........3 K6
River St *DERBY* DE1........2 C1
River Vw *BPR/DUF* DE56........12 A3
Robert St *DERBY* DE1........2 E2
Robin Croft Rd *DERBYW* DE22.....25 H4
Robinia Cl *DERBYE* DE21........28 B5
Robin Rd *DERBYW* DE22........34 A4
Robinscross *BWSH/BRSTN* DE72...45 G5
Robinson's Hl *MELB/CHEL* DE73 ...75 G4
Robson Cl *DERBYSE* DE24........53 H2
Roby Lea *CDON/KEG* DE74........72 C3
Rochester Cl *DERBYE* DE24........53 H4
Rochley Cl *DERBYE* DE21........27 C5
The Rockery *DERBYE* DE21........19 F1
Rockbourne Cl *DERBYSE* DE24.....54 C3
Rockhouse Rd *DERBYE* DE21........53 H3
Rockingham Cl *DERBYW* DE22......26 B4
Rodsley Crs *NORM/LIT* DE23........51 G4
Roe Farm La *DERBYE* DE21........35 F4
Roehampton Dr *DERBYW* DE22.....32 C4
Roe Wk *NORM/LIT* DE23........42 B4
Roman Cl *DERBY* DE1........34 C4
Roman Wy *BWSH/BRSTN* DE72....45 H5
Romsley Cl *MCKLVR* DE3........40 A2
Rona Cl *DERBYSE* DE24........51 H5
Ronald Cl *NORM/LIT* DE23........50 B2
Roosevelt Av *DERBYE* DE21........36 A5

The Ropewalk *ILK* DE7 ....21 G4
Rosamond's Ride
  NORM/LIT DE23.....................51 G1
Rose Av *BWSH/BRSTN* DE72........45 H5
Roseberry Ct *DERBYE* DE21........36 A2
Rosedale Av *DERBYE* DE24........53 H3
Roseheath Cl *NORM/LIT* DE23......51 H4
Rose Hill St *NORM/LIT* DE23........42 B4
Rose La *MELB/CHEL* DE73........74 B5
Rosemary Dr *DERBYSE* DE24.......53 H4
Rosemoor La *DERBYE* DE21........36 A2
Rosemount Ct *DERBYW* DE22......25 F5
Rosengrave St *DERBY* DE1........2 B6
Rosette Ct *DERBYE* DE21........28 B5
Rosewood Cl *DERBYSE* DE24........54 B2
Rossington Dr *NORM/LIT* DE23.....50 C3
Rosslyn Gdns *DERBYSE* DE24........53 H3
Rothbury Pl *DERBYE* DE21........35 F2
Rothesay Ct *BWSH/BRSTN* DE72...51 H5
Rothwell La *BPR/DUF* DE56........6 C3
Rothwell Rd *MCKLVR* DE3........40 A3
Rough Heanor Rd *MCKLVR* DE3...40 A3
Roughton Cl *MCKLVR* DE3........50 A1
Roundhouse Rd *DERBYSE* DE24....3 H6
Routh Av *CDON/KEG* DE74........73 E5
Rowan Cl *DERBYE* DE21........44 A1
  DERBYE DE24..........................61 G1
Rowan Dr *BPR/DUF* DE56........14 A2
Rowan Park Cl *NORM/LIT* DE23....51 G2
Rowdtich Av *DERBYW* DE22........41 G3
Rowdtich Pl *DERBYW* DE22........41 G3
Rowena Ct *DERBYSE* DE24........53 G2
Rowland St *DERBYSE* DE24........53 F3
Rowley Gdns *NORM/LIT* DE23......51 F2
Rowley La *NORM/LIT* DE23........51 F2
Rowsley Av *NORM/LIT* DE23........51 G1
Roxburgh Av *DERBYE* DE21........35 F4
Royal Ap *MELB/CHEL* DE73........63 G4
Royal Cl *BWSH/BRSTN* DE72........45 G5
Royal Ga *BPR/DUF* DE56........7 E4
Royal Gv *DERBYE* DE21........28 C5
Royal Hill Rd *DERBYE* DE21........36 C5
Royal Wy *DERBYSE* DE24........43 F3
Roydon Cl *MCKLVR* DE3........39 H2
Royston Dr *BPR/DUF* DE56........7 E2
Rudyard Av *DERBYE* DE21........44 D1
Ruffstone Cl *BPR/DUF* DE56........12 D3
Rupert Rd *DERBYE* DE21........35 H4
Rushcliffe Av *DERBYE* DE21........35 G5
Rushcliffe Gdns *DERBYE* DE21.....35 G5
Rushdale Av *NORM/LIT* DE23......51 G3
Rushup Cl *DERBYW* DE22........26 B3
Rydal Cl *DERBYW* DE22........25 H4
Ryde Houses *DERBYSE* DE24......54 B2
Rye Butts *MELB/CHEL* DE73........63 H3
Rye Cl *DERBYE* DE21........27 F5
Ryedale Gdns *NORM/LIT* DE23.....51 H5
Ryegrass Cl *BPR/DUF* DE56........7 E4
Ryegrass Rd *DERBYE* DE21........36 B1
Rykneld Cl *NORM/LIT* DE23........50 B3
Rykneld Dr *NORM/LIT* DE23........50 B2
Rykneld Rd *NORM/LIT* DE23........50 B3
Rykneld Wy *NORM/LIT* DE23........50 B3
Rykneld Hl *RIPLEY* DE5........8 A5
Rymill Rd *BPR/DUF* DE56........14 A3
Rymill Dr *DERBYE* DE21........35 G2

S

Sacheveral St *DERBY* DE1........2 D6
Sacheverel St *DERBY* DE1........2 C6
Sackville St *NORM/LIT* DE23........52 A1
Sadler Ga *DERBY* DE1........2 C3
Saffron Dr *DERBYE* DE21........35 H2
St Agnes Av *DERBYW* DE22........25 G4
St Albans Rd *DERBYW* DE22........41 F3
St Alkmund's Cl *BPR/DUF* DE56...17 H1
St Alkmunds Wy *BPR/DUF* DE56...17 H1
  DERBY DE1............................2 D2
St Andrews Vw *DERBYE* DE21.....35 F3
St Annes Cl *DERBY* DE1........33 H5
St Anne's La *CDON/KEG* DE74 .....73 E4
St Augustine St *NORM/LIT* DE23...42 A5
St Bride's Wk *DERBYW* DE22........33 E5

St Chad's Rd *NORM/LIT* DE23........41 H4
St Clare's Cl *NORM/LIT* DE23........41 G4
St Cuthbert's Rd *DERBYW* DE22 ...41 F3
St David's Cl *DERBYW* DE22........41 G3
St Edmund's Cl *DERBYW* DE22 ...26 A4
St Edward's Rd *CDON/KEG* DE74...73 E5
St Georges Est *DERBYE* DE21........3 H1
St George's Pl *BPR/DUF* DE56......6 A3
St Giles Rd *NORM/LIT* DE23........42 A5
St Helen's St *DERBY* DE1........2 B2
St Hugh's Cl *DERBYW* DE22........34 A1
St James Chambers *DERBY* DE1....2 C3
St James Cl *BPR/DUF* DE56........7 E3
St James Ct *DERBY* DE1........1 H1
St James' Rd *NORM/LIT* DE23......42 A5
St James's St *DERBY* DE1........2 C4
St James St *DERBY* DE1........2 C4
  NORM/LIT DE23......................42 B5
St John's Av *DERBYE* DE21........44 A1
St John's Cl *DERBYE* DE22........25 G5
St John's Dr *BPR/DUF* DE56........13 H2
St John's Rd *BPR/DUF* DE56........6 B3
  ILK DE7...............................15 G5
St Mark's Rd *DERBYE* DE21........35 E4
St Mary's Av *BWSH/BRSTN* DE72...56 D2
St Marys Br *DERBY* DE1........2 D1
St Mary's Cl *DERBYSE* DE24........53 H3
St Mary's Ct *DERBY* DE1........2 C1
St Marys Wharf Rd *DERBY* DE1....34 C4
St Matthew's Wk *DERBYW* DE22...34 A1
St Mawes Cl *DERBYW* DE22........25 G4
St Mellion *MCKLVR* DE3........40 C5
St Michaels *DERBY* DE1........2 C2
St Michael's Cl *BPR/DUF* DE56.....12 D4
  DERBYSE DE24......................54 B2
St Michaels Ct *DERBY* DE1........2 C2
St Michael's La *DERBY* DE1........2 C2
St Michaels Vw *DERBYSE* DE24....54 B2
St Nicholas Cl *DERBYW* DE22........33 G1
St Nicholas Ms *DERBY* DE1........34 A4
St Pancras Wy *DERBY* DE1........2 D1
St Pauls Rd *DERBY* DE1........34 B4
St Peter's Churchyard
  DERBY DE1.........................2 D5
St Peter's Cl *BPR/DUF* DE56........6 A3
St Peters Cft *BPR/DUF* DE56........6 A3
St Peter's Rd *MELB/CHEL* DE73 ...63 H4
St Peter's St *DERBY* DE1........2 D5
St Peters Wy *DERBY* DE1........2 D5
St Quentin Cl *NORM/LIT* DE23......41 F3
St Ronan's Av *BPR/DUF* DE56......17 H2
St Stephens Cl
  BWSH/BRSTN DE72.................45 G5
  NORM/LIT DE23.....................51 G3
St Swithin's Cl *DERBYW* DE22......41 F3
St Thomas Rd *NORM/LIT* DE23 ....42 B5
St Werburgh's Vw
  DERBYE DE21.........................44 C1
St Wystan's Rd *DERBYW* DE22 ....41 F3
Sale St *NORM/LIT* DE23........42 C4
Salisbury Dr *BPR/DUF* DE56........7 E2
Salisbury La *MELB/CHEL* DE73.....76 A3
Salisbury St *NORM/LIT* DE23........42 B3
Sallywood Cl *DERBYSE* DE24........61 G2
Saltburn Cl *DERBYE* DE21........34 D2
Salter Cl *CDON/KEG* DE74........72 C3
Samantha Ct *DERBYE* DE21........36 A2
Sancroft Av *DERBYE* DE21........36 D5
Sancroft Rd *DERBYE* DE21........37 E5
Sandalwood Cl *DERBYSE* DE24 ....54 B2
Sandbach Cl *DERBYE* DE21........35 H2
Sandbed La *BPR/DUF* DE56........6 D5
Sanderling Heath *MCKLVR* DE3....49 G3
Sanderson Rd *DERBYE* DE21........36 A5
Sandfield Cl *DERBYE* DE21........36 A3
Sandgate Cl *DERBYW* DE22........54 A3
Sandown Av *MCKLVR* DE3........39 H3
Sandown Rd *DERBYSE* DE24........53 E1
Sandringham Dr *DERBYE* DE21....45 E2
Sandringham Rd *DERBYE* DE21 ...35 F2
Sandyhill Cl *MELB/CHEL* DE73.....63 H2
Sandy La *DERBYE* DE21........19 G1
Sandypits La *RDERBYSW* DE65....48 B5
Santolina Dr *DERBYE* DE21........35 G2
Sapperton Cl *NORM/LIT* DE23......51 G4
Saundersfoot Wy *DERBYE* DE21...36 A1
Save Penny La *BPR/DUF* DE56.....12 B5
Sawley Rd *BWSH/BRSTN* DE72 ....57 E2
Saxondale Av *MCKLVR* DE3........39 H2
Scarborough Ri *DERBYE* DE21......35 E2
Scarcliffe Cl *DERBYSE* DE24........63 F1
Scarsdale Av *DERBYW* DE22........25 F5
  NORM/LIT DE23......................41 F4
Scarsdale Rd *BPR/DUF* DE56......17 H2
School La *CDON/KEG* DE74........72 D3
  MELB/CHEL DE73....................63 H3
The Scotches *BPR/DUF* DE56......6 A2

Scott Dr *BPR/DUF* DE56........7
Scott St *NORM/LIT* DE23........42
Seagrave Cl *DERBYE* DE21........36
Seale St *DERBY* DE1........34
Searl St *DERBY* DE1........2
Seascale Cl *DERBYE* DE21........35
Seaton Cl *MCKLVR* DE3........39
Second Av *BWSH/BRSTN* DE72 47
  MELB/CHEL DE73...................63
Sedgebrook Cl *DERBYE* DE21......35
Sedgemoor Wy *NORM/LIT* DE23...50
Sefton Rd *DERBYE* DE21........35
Selborne St *DERBYSE* DE24........43
Selina Cl *CDON/KEG* DE74........72
Selina St *MELB/CHEL* DE73........75
Selkirk St *DERBYE* DE21........35
Selworthy Cl *DERBYE* DE21........35
Selwyn St *DERBYW* DE22........33
Serina Av *NORM/LIT* DE23........51
The Settlement
  BWSH/BRSTN DE72.................45
Sevenlands Dr *DERBYSE* DE24.....54
Sevenoaks Av *DERBYW* DE22 40
Severnale Cl *DERBYW* DE22........26
Severn St *DERBYSE* DE24........53
Seymour Cl *DERBYSE* DE24........41
Shacklecross Cl
  BWSH/BRSTN DE72.................45
Shaftesbury Crs
  NORM/LIT DE23.....................42
Shaftesbury St
  NORM/LIT DE23.....................42
Shaftesbury St South
  NORM/LIT DE23.....................42
Shakespeare St *DERBYSE* DE24...52
Shaldon Dr *NORM/LIT* DE23........41
Shalfleet Dr *DERBYSE* DE24........54
Shamrock St *NORM/LIT* DE23......41
Shandwick Ct *DERBYSE* DE24 61
Shanklin Houses
  DERBYSE DE24......................54
Shannon Cl *NORM/LIT* DE23........51
Shannon Houses
  DERBYSE DE24......................53
Shardlow Rd
  BWSH/BRSTN DE72.................65
  DERBYSE DE24......................54
Shaw La *BPR/DUF* DE56........12
Shaws Gn *DERBYW* DE22........33
Shaw St *DERBYW* DE22........33
Shaw's Yd *BPR/DUF* DE56........13
Sheffield Pl *DERBY* DE1........3
Sheldon Rd *HEANOR* DE75........9
Shelford Cl *MCKLVR* DE3........39
Shelley Dr *DERBYSE* DE24........52
Shelmory Cl *DERBYSE* DE24........53
Shelton Dr *DERBYSE* DE24........63
Shenington Wy *DERBYE* DE21......36
Shepherd's La *MELB/CHEL* DE73...75
Shepherd St *NORM/LIT* DE23......41
Sherbourne Dr *BPR/DUF* DE56.....7
Sheridan St *DERBYSE* DE24........52
Sherston Cl *DERBYE* DE21........36
Sherwin St *DERBYW* DE22........33
Sherwood Av
  BWSH/BRSTN DE72.................45
  DERBYE DE21........................35
  NORM/LIT DE23.....................51
Sherwood St *DERBYW* DE22........41
Shetland Cl *DERBYE* DE21........34
Shields Crs *CDON/KEG* DE74.......72
Shiregate Gdns *NORM/LIT* DE23 ..50
Shireoaks *BPR/DUF* DE56........5
Shireoaks Cl *NORM/LIT* DE23......51
Shirley Cl *CDON/KEG* DE74........72
Shirley Crs *BWSH/BRSTN* DE72 ...57
Shirley Pk *BWSH/BRSTN* DE72.....65
Shirley Rd *DERBYE* DE21........35
Shop Stones *BWSH/BRSTN* DE72..45
Short Av *DERBYW* DE22........26
Short Hl *MELB/CHEL* DE73........76
Short Lands *BPR/DUF* DE56........6
Short La *CDON/KEG* DE74........72
Short St *BPR/DUF* DE56........6
Shorwell Gdns *DERBYSE* DE24.....54
Shrewsbury Cl *DERBYE* DE21......36
Shropshire Av *DERBYE* DE21.......35
The Shrubberies
  NORM/LIT DE23.....................42
Siddals La *DERBYW* DE21........26
Siddals Rd *DERBY* DE1........3
Siddons St *DERBYSE* DE24........53
The Sidings *DERBYE* DE21........43
Sidmouth Cl *DERBYSE* DE24........54
Sidney St *DERBY* DE1........42
Silverburn Dr *DERBYE* DE21........35
Silverdale Cl *MELB/CHEL* DE73 ...63
Silverhill Rd *DERBYE* DE21........34

ilver Hill Rd *NORM/LIT* DE23......42 B4
ilver La *BWSH/BRSTN* DE72......55 E4
ilverton Dr *DERBYSE* DE24......61 F2
imcoe Leys *DERBYE* DE73......63 G3
imon Fields Cl *ILK* DE7......21 F3
ims Av *DERBY* DE1......41 H1
inclair Cl *DERBYSE* DE24......51 H5
infin Av *DERBYE* DE21......44 C2
infin Fields Crs *DERBYSE* DE24......53 E4
infin La *DERBYSE* DE24......52 A5
  MELB/CHEL DE73......68 B1
infin Moor La *DERBYSE* DE24......62 A1
ir Frank Whittle Rd
  DERBYSE DE24......34 D4
iskin Cl *MCKLVR* DE3......49 C2
iskin Dr *DERBYSE* DE24......51 G5
ister's La *BWSH/BRSTN* DE72......45 H1
itwell Cl *DERBYE* DE21......44 C2
itwell St *BPR/DUF* DE56......13 H3
itwell St *DERBY* DE1......2 D5
  DERBYE DE21......44 C2
kiddaw Dr *MCKLVR* DE3......40 B5
kylark Wy *DERBYSE* DE24......51 G5
lack La *DERBYW* DE22......34 A1
lade Cl *RDERBYSW* DE65......48 B5
lade Lands Dr
  MELB/CHEL DE73......63 H2
lade La *MELB/CHEL* DE73......77 E4
laidburn Cl *MCKLVR* DE3......40 H5
laney Cl *DERBYSE* DE24......53 F2
laney Houses *DERBYSE* * DE24......53 F4
later Av *DERBYW* DE22......41 H1
ledmere Cl *DERBYSE* DE24......54 B2
leepy La *MELB/CHEL* DE73......76 A1
lindon Cft *DERBYSE* DE24......54 C3
loane Rd *DERBYW* DE22......32 D5
malley Dr *DERBYW* DE22......28 A5
malley Mill Rd *ILK* DE7......20 C1
mall Meer Cl *MELB/CHEL* DE73......63 G3
mith Av *MELB/CHEL* DE73......76 A2
nake La *BPR/DUF* DE56......17 G2
nelsmoor La *MELB/CHEL* DE73......64 C2
nelston Crs *NORM/LIT* DE23......41 F4
nowberry Av *BPR/DUF* DE56......6 C5
ociety Pl *NORM/LIT* DE23......42 H4
olway Cl *DERBYE* DE21......35 H1
omerby Wy *DERBYSE* DE24......35 G1
omersal Cl *DERBYSE* DE24......63 F1
omerset St *DERBYE* DE21......35 E4
omme Rd *DERBYW* DE22......25 E5
outh Av *DERBYE* DE21......44 D2
  DERBYW DE22......26 B5
  MELB/CHEL DE73......63 G1
  NORM/LIT DE23......41 F4
outh Brae Cl *NORM/LIT* DE23......51 G2
outhcroft *NORM/LIT* DE23......51 G4
outhdown Cl *DERBYSE* DE24......61 F2
outh Dr *DERBY* DE1......34 A4
  DERBYE DE21......43 H1
  MCKLVR DE3......40 D4
  MELB/CHEL DE73......63 G1
outhgate Cl *MCKLVR* DE3......39 H3
outhmead Wy *DERBYW* DE22......41 E3
outh St *BWSH/BRSTN* DE72......56 D2
  DERBY DE1......2 C3
  MELB/CHEL DE73......75 H3
outhwark Cl *DERBYW* DE22......41 E1
outhwood St *DERBYSE* DE24......53 F1
overeign Wy *DERBYE* DE21......28 C5
  HEANOR DE75......15 H1
owter Rd *DERBY* DE1......2 D2
pa La *DERBY* DE1......2 B7
parrow Cl *DERBYSE* DE24......51 G5
peedwell Cl *DERBYE* DE21......28 B5
penbeck Dr *DERBYW* DE22......26 B3
pencer Av *BPR/DUF* DE56......6 C3
  DERBYSE DE24......53 E5
pencer Rd *BPR/DUF* DE56......6 B3
pencer St *DERBYSE* DE24......53 E5
  ILK DE7......21 E3
pindletree Dr *DERBYE* DE21......35 F1
pinners Wy *BPR/DUF* DE56......6 D1
The Spinney *BPR/DUF* DE56......6 B1
  BWSH/BRSTN DE72......45 H5
  CDON/KEG DE74......72 D4
pinney Cl *DERBYW* DE22......34 B1
pinney Hl *MELB/CHEL* DE73......75 H3
pinney Rd *DERBYE* DE21......35 G4
  DERBYW DE22......41 H3
pittal *CDON/KEG* DE74......72 D3
pooney Wood Ct
  NORM/LIT * DE23......50 C2
The Spot *DERBY* * DE1......2 D5
pring Cl *BPR/DUF* DE56......5 H1
  BWSH/BRSTN DE72......57 F1
pringdale Cl *MCKLVR* DE3......40 B5

Springfield *NORM/LIT* DE23......41 E4
Springfield Av *HEANOR* DE75......9 G2
Springfield Dr *BPR/DUF* DE56......17 G2
Springfield Rd *DERBYE* DE21......44 A1
  MELB/CHEL DE73......63 F2
  RDERBYSW DE65......58 A1
Spring Gdns *DERBYE* DE21......35 G4
Spring Hollow *BPR/DUF* DE56......11 F5
Spring St *DERBY* DE1......2 A6
Springwood Dr *DERBYE* DE21......35 H1
The Square *DERBYW* DE22......34 B2
  MCKLVR DE3......40 A5
Squires Wy *NORM/LIT* DE23......50 D3
Stables St *DERBYW* DE22......41 G1
Stadium Vw *DERBYSE* DE24......43 F3
Stafford Cl *ILK* DE7......15 E4
Stafford St *DERBY* DE1......2 A4
Staines Cl *MCKLVR* DE3......39 H4
Stainsby Av *ILK* DE7......14 D4
Staker La *MCKLVR* DE3......50 A3
Stamford St *DERBYSE* DE24......53 E3
Stanage Gn *MCKLVR* DE3......40 C4
Stanhope Rd *MCKLVR* DE3......40 B5
Stanhope St *NORM/LIT* DE23......42 A5
Stanier Wy *DERBYE* DE21......43 H3
Stanley Cl *DERBYW* DE22......34 A3
Stanley Rd *DERBYE* DE21......43 H1
  DERBYSE DE24......53 F3
Stanley St *DERBYW* DE22......41 G1
Stanstead Av *MELB/CHEL* DE73......39 H2
Stanton Av *BPR/DUF* DE56......6 C3
Stanton Hl *MELB/CHEL* DE73......74 D5
Stanton St *NORM/LIT* DE23......42 A5
Starcross Ct *MCKLVR* DE3......39 H3
Starkie Av *CDON/KEG* DE74......72 C4
Statham St *DERBYW* DE22......33 H4
Station Ap *BPR/DUF* DE56......18 A1
  DERBY DE1......3 F5
Station Cl *MELB/CHEL* DE73......63 G1
Station La *RIPLEY* DE5......9 C1
Station Rd *BPR/DUF* DE56......18 A1
  BWSH/BRSTN DE72......45 C3
  BWSH/BRSTN DE72......57 E2
  CDON/KEG DE74......73 E1
  DERBYE DE21......26 D1
  DERBYE DE21......44 C3
  ILK DE7......27 E4
  ILK DE7......29 C3
  MCKLVR DE3......40 A4
  MELB/CHEL DE73......63 C3
  MELB/CHEL DE73......76 A2
  RIPLEY DE5......8 A4
Staunton Av *NORM/LIT* DE23......51 H1
Staunton Cl *CDON/KEG* DE74......72 D3
Staveley Cl *DERBYSE* DE24......63 F1
Staverton Dr *MCKLVR* DE3......40 A2
Steeple Cl *DERBYE* DE21......35 F1
Stenson Av *NORM/LIT* DE23......51 H3
Stenson Rd *DERBYSE* DE24......61 F2
Stephensons Wy *DERBYE* DE21......43 H5
Stepping Cl *DERBYW* DE22......41 G1
Stepping La *DERBYW* DE22......41 G1
Sterling Cl *RIPLEY* DE5......8 A5
Stevenage Cl *DERBYSE* DE24......53 G4
Stevens La *BWSH/BRSTN* DE72......57 G1
Stevenson Av
  BWSH/BRSTN DE72......57 E1
Stevenson Pl *NORM/LIT* DE23......51 H1
Stewart Cl *DERBYE* DE21......36 D5
Stiles Rd *DERBYSE* DE24......54 D5
Stirling Cl *DERBYE* DE21......34 D3
Stockbrook Rd *DERBYW* DE22......41 G3
Stockbrook St *DERBYW* DE22......41 H3
Stockdove Cl *DERBYSE* DE24......51 G5
Stocker Av *DERBYSE* DE24......54 B2
Stoke Cl *BPR/DUF* DE56......7 E3
Stonechat Cl *MCKLVR* DE3......40 D3
Stone Cl *DERBYE* DE21......36 D5
Stonehill *CDON/KEG* DE74......73 E5
Stone Hill Rd *NORM/LIT* DE23......42 A4
Stonesby Cl *DERBYE* DE21......35 G1
Stoney Cross *DERBYE* DE21......44 D3
Stoneyfield Bank
  BPR/DUF DE56......6 B2
Stoney Flatts Crs *DERBYE* DE21......35 H5
Stoney Gate Rd *DERBYE* DE21......44 C3
Stoney La *DERBYW* DE22......41 D1
Stonyhurst Ct *DERBYE* DE21......63 F1
Stony La *BPR/DUF* DE56......12 D4
Stoodley Pike Gdns
  DERBYW DE22......33 F1
Stores Rd *DERBYE* DE21......34 C4
Stornoway Cl *DERBYSE* DE24......61 G1
Stourport Dr *MELB/CHEL* DE73......63 H1
Stowmarket Dr *DERBYE* DE21......35 E2
The Strand *DERBY* * DE1......2 C3
Strand *DERBY* DE1......2 C3
Strand Ar *DERBY* * DE1......2 C3

Stratford Rd *DERBYE* DE21......35 E1
Strathaven Ct *DERBYE* DE21......44 D1
Strathmore Av *DERBYSE* DE24......53 G3
Streatham Rd *DERBYW* DE22......32 D5
Street La *RIPLEY* DE5......7 H1
Stretton Cl *MCKLVR* DE3......40 A5
Stroma Cl *DERBYSE* DE24......61 G1
Strutt St *BPR/DUF* DE56......6 A4
  NORM/LIT DE23......42 B4
Stuart St *DERBY* DE1......2 D2
Studbrook Cl *CDON/KEG* DE74......72 C4
Sturges La *BWSH/BRSTN* DE72......55 E5
Sudbury Cl *DERBYE* DE21......44 D1
Sudbury Dr *DERBY* DE1......41 H1
Suffolk Av *DERBYSE* DE24......53 G3
Sulleys Fld *DERBYW* DE22......25 G1
Summerbrook Ct *DERBYW* DE22......2 A6
Summer Wood Ct
  NORM/LIT DE23......51 G2
Sunart Cl *DERBYSE* DE24......61 G1
Sundew Cl *DERBYE* DE21......45 E2
Sundown Av *NORM/LIT* DE23......51 G3
Sunningdale Av *DERBYE* DE21......44 C1
Sunny Bank Gdns
  BPR/DUF DE56......6 A5
Sunny Gv *DERBYE* DE21......43 H1
Sunny Hl *BPR/DUF* DE56......12 A3
Sunnyhill Av *NORM/LIT* DE23......51 H3
Sun St *DERBYW* DE22......2 A6
Surbiton Cl *DERBYW* DE22......32 D5
Surrey St *DERBYW* DE22......33 G3
Sussex Circ *DERBYE* DE21......35 F3
Sutherland Rd *NORM/LIT* DE23......52 A1
Sutton Av *MELB/CHEL* DE73......63 G1
Sutton Cl *DERBYW* DE22......33 G3
Sutton Dr *DERBYSE* DE24......53 F5
Sutton La *RDERBYSW* DE65......48 A4
Swallow Cl *MCKLVR* DE3......40 D3
Swallowdale Rd *DERBYSE* DE24......51 G5
Swan Hl *MCKLVR* DE3......49 G3
Swanmore Rd *NORM/LIT* DE23......50 D1
Swanwick *DERBYE* DE21......35 H2
Swarkestone Br
  MELB/CHEL DE73......69 E2
Swarkestone Dr
  NORM/LIT DE23......51 F4
Swarkestone Rd
  MELB/CHEL DE73......68 C1
Swayfield Cl *MCKLVR* DE3......39 G3
Sweetbriar Cl *DERBYSE* DE24......53 H4
Swift Cl *MCKLVR* DE5......40 D5
Swinburne St *DERBY* DE1......2 C7
Swinderby Dr *DERBYE* DE21......36 A2
Swinney Bank *BPR/DUF* DE56......6 B2
Swinney La *BPR/DUF* DE56......6 B2
Sycamore Av *DERBYW* DE22......25 G5
  RDERBYSW DE65......60 A2
Sycamore Cl *RDERBYSW* DE65......48 B5
Sycamore Ct *DERBYE* DE21......44 D1
Sycamore Rd *CDON/KEG* DE74......73 E2
Sydenham Rd *DERBYW* DE22......32 D4
Sydney Cl *MCKLVR* DE3......40 C3
Sydney Houses
  NORM/LIT * DE23......41 F5
Sydney Rd *BWSH/BRSTN* DE72......56 D2

Taddington Rd *DERBYE* DE21......35 F3
Talbot St *DERBYW* DE22......2 A4
Talgarth Cl *DERBYE* DE21......36 B1
Tamar Av *DERBYW* DE22......25 G4
Tamworth Rd
  BWSH/BRSTN DE72......67 G4
Tamworth St *BPR/DUF* DE56......17 H2
Tansley Av *ILK* DE7......21 F4
Tansley Ri *DERBYE* DE21......35 G2
Tants Meadow *BPR/DUF* DE56......13 H4
Tantum Av *HEANOR* DE75......9 H3
Tanyard Cl *CDON/KEG* DE74......73 E3
Taplow Cl *MCKLVR* DE3......39 H4
Tarina Cl *MELB/CHEL* DE73......63 H3
Tasman Cl *MCKLVR* DE3......40 C3
Taunton Cl *DERBYSE* DE24......54 B1
Taverners Crs *NORM/LIT* DE23......51 G1
Tavistock Cl *DERBYSE* DE24......61 G1
Tawny Wy *NORM/LIT* DE23......50 D2
Tay Cl *DERBYSE* DE24......61 G2
Taylor St *DERBYSE* DE24......43 E4
Tay La *DERBYE* DE21......61 G1
Tay Wk *DERBYW* DE22......25 H5
Tedworth Av *DERBYSE* DE24......61 G2
Telford Cl *MCKLVR* DE3......40 B5
Templar Cl *DERBYSE* DE24......61 F2
Templebell Cl *NORM/LIT* DE23......50 D3
Temple St *NORM/LIT* DE23......42 A3

Tenby Dr *DERBYE* DE21......36 B1
Tennessee Rd *DERBYE* DE21......35 H4
Tennyson St *DERBYSE* DE24......53 E2
The Terrace *DERBYE* * DE21......35 F4
Terry Pl *DERBYSE* DE24......53 C2
Teviot Pl *DERBYE* DE21......35 H1
Tewkesbury Crs *DERBYE* DE21......35 E3
Thackeray St *DERBYSE* DE24......52 B4
Thames Cl *DERBYW* DE22......40 C1
Thanet Dr *DERBYSE* DE24......53 H3
Thatch Cl *DERBYW* DE22......34 A1
Theatre Wk *DERBY* DE1......2 E4
Thirlmere Av *DERBYW* DE22......25 H5
Thirsk Pl *DERBYSE* DE24......53 C2
Thistledown Cl *DERBYW* DE22......34 B1
Thomas Cook Cl
  MELB/CHEL DE73......75 H3
Thomas Ct *DERBY* * DE1......41 G2
Thore Cl *DERBYE* DE21......35 H2
Thoresby Crs
  BWSH/BRSTN DE72......56 C2
Thorn Cl *DERBYW* DE22......25 G4
Thorndike Av *DERBYSE* DE24......53 H2
Thorndon Cl *MCKLVR* DE3......50 A1
Thorness *DERBYSE* DE24......54 B4
Thornhill Rd *NORM/LIT* DE23......41 F5
Thorn St *NORM/LIT* DE23......42 A4
Thorntree La *DERBY* DE1......2 D4
Thorpe Dr *MCKLVR* DE3......40 B3
Thorpelands Dr *DERBYW* DE22......33 H2
Thorpe Wy *BPR/DUF* DE56......6 C2
Thrushton Cl *RDERBYSW* DE65......59 H2
Thruxton Cl *DERBYSE* DE24......54 B3
Thurcroft Cl *DERBYW* DE22......33 F5
Thurlow Ct *DERBYE* DE21......35 H2
Thurstone Furlong
  MELB/CHEL DE73......63 F3
Tiber Cl *DERBYSE* DE24......54 C4
Tickham Av *DERBYSE* DE24......61 F2
Ticknall La *RIPLEY* DE5......14 A1
Tideswell Rd *DERBYE* DE21......35 C2
Tilbury Pl *DERBYSE* DE24......53 H4
Tiller Cl *NORM/LIT* DE23......51 E3
Timbersbrook Cl *DERBYE* DE21......35 H2
Timsbury Ct *DERBYE* DE21......35 F1
Tintagel Cl *NORM/LIT* DE23......42 C4
Tipnall Rd *CDON/KEG* DE74......72 D4
Tiree Cl *DERBYSE* DE24......52 A5
Tissington Dr *DERBYE* DE21......28 A5
Tiverton Cl *MCKLVR* DE3......40 A2
Tivoli Gdns *DERBYW* DE22......33 H4
Tobermory Wy *DERBYSE* DE24......61 G1
Tomlinsons Cottages
  DERBYE * DE21......34 D1
Tonbridge Dr *DERBYSE* DE24......53 H4
Top Farm Ct *BPR/DUF* DE56......13 G2
Top Manor Cl
  BWSH/BRSTN DE72......45 H1
Torridon Cl *DERBYSE* DE24......51 H5
Tower St *DERBYSE* DE24......53 E2
Towle Cl *BWSH/BRSTN* DE72......45 G5
Towles Pastures
  CDON/KEG DE74......72 D4
The Town *DERBYE* DE21......26 D1
Town End Rd
  BWSH/BRSTN DE72......57 E2
Townsend Gv *MELB/CHEL* DE73......63 H4
Town St *BPR/DUF* DE56......12 D4
  BPR/DUF DE56......17 H2
Traffic St *DERBY* DE1......2 E4
Trafford Wy *NORM/LIT* DE23......51 F1
Tredegar Dr *DERBYE* DE21......36 A1
Trefoil Cl *NORM/LIT* DE23......50 D2
Tregaron Cl *DERBYE* DE21......36 B1
Tregony Wy *DERBYSE* DE24......61 G2
Trent Bridge Ct *NORM/LIT* DE23......51 F1
Trent Cl *DERBYSE* DE24......61 G2
Trent Dr *NORM/LIT* DE23......51 G4
Trent La *BWSH/BRSTN* DE72......70 D3
  CDON/KEG DE74......72 D3
  MELB/CHEL DE73......70 B5
Trenton Green Dr
  DERBYE DE21......36 A5
Trent Ri *DERBYE* DE21......45 E2
Trent St *DERBYSE* DE24......53 E2
Tresillian Cl *DERBYW* DE22......33 H1
Treveris Cl *DERBYW* DE22......44 D2
Trinity St *DERBY* DE1......3 F6
Trocadero Ct *DERBY* * DE1......2 D7
Troon Cl *NORM/LIT* DE23......50 D1
Troutbeck Gv *NORM/LIT* DE23......50 D2
Trowbridge Cl *DERBYE* DE21......35 F1
Trowels La *DERBYW* DE22......41 F2
Truro Crs *DERBYE* DE21......35 F3
Trusley Gdns *NORM/LIT* DE23......51 G4
Tudor Field Cl *MELB/CHEL* DE73......63 H3
Tudor Rd *DERBYE* DE21......35 H5
Tufnell Gdns *DERBYW* DE22......33 E4

Tulla Cl *DERBYSE* DE24 ......61 H2
Tuphall Cl *MELB/CHEL* DE73 ......63 H2
Turner St *MELB/CHEL* DE24 ......53 E3
Tuxford Cl *DERBYE* DE21 ......36 A2
Tweeds Muir Cl *DERBYE* DE21 ......35 G1
Twickenham Dr *DERBYW* DE22 ......32 D5
Twin Oaks Cl *NORM/LIT* DE23 ......50 C1
Twyford Cl *HEANOR* DE75 ......15 H2
Twyford Rd *MELB/CHEL* DE73 ......68 B1
Twyford St *NORM/LIT* DE23 ......42 B3
Tyndale Cha *DERBYSE* DE24 ......61 H2

U

Uffa Magna *MCKLVR* DE3 ......49 H1
Ullswater Cl *DERBYE* DE21 ......35 E1
Ullswater Dr *DERBYE* DE21 ......36 D5
Underhill Av *NORM/LIT* DE23 ......52 A5
Underhill Cl *NORM/LIT* DE23 ......51 H3
Union St *MELB/CHEL* DE73 ......75 H3
Uplands Av *NORM/LIT* DE23 ......51 F3
Uplands Gdns *NORM/LIT* DE23 ......41 H4
Upper Bainbrigge St
   NORM/LIT DE23 ......42 A4
Upper Boundary Rd
   DERBYW DE22 ......41 H2
Upper Dale Rd *NORM/LIT* DE23 ......42 A5
Upper Hall Cl *BPR/DUF* DE56 ......12 D4
Upper Hollow *DERBYE* DE21 ......41 F5
Upper Marehay Rd *RIPLEY* DE5 ......8 B1
Upper Moor Rd *DERBYSE* DE24 ......53 F3
Uttoxeter New Rd
   DERBYW DE22 ......41 F3
Uttoxeter Old Rd
   DERBYW DE22 ......41 G2
Uttoxeter Rd *MCKLVR* DE3 ......40 A5

V

Vale Mills *DERBYW* DE22 * 2 A7
Valerie Rd *BWSH/BRSTN* DE72 ......65 E5
Valley Rd *DERBYE* DE21 ......36 A5
   NORM/LIT DE23 ......41 G5
Valley Vw *BPR/DUF* DE56 ......6 B5
Valley View Dr *ILK* DE7 ......21 F4
Vancouver Av *DERBYE* DE21 ......44 C5
Varley St *DERBYSE* DE24 ......53 E2
Vauxhall Av *DERBYW* DE22 ......32 D4
Ventor Houses *DERBYSE* DE24 * 54 B2
Verbena Dr *NORM/LIT* DE23 ......51 C5
Vermont Dr *DERBYE* DE21 ......36 B5
Vernon Dr *DERBYE* DE21 ......45 E2
Vernon St *DERBY* DE1 ......41 H1
Vestry Rd *DERBYE* DE21 ......35 F1
Vetchfield Cl *DERBYSE* DE24 ......62 A2
Vicarage Av *NORM/LIT* DE23 ......41 H4
Vicarage Cl *BPR/DUF* DE56 ......6 B3
   ILK DE7 ......15 F4
Vicarage Ct *MCKLVR* DE3 ......40 A5
Vicarage Dr *DERBYE* DE21 ......35 H4
Vicarage La *BPR/DUF* DE56 ......17 H1
   DERBYE DE21 ......18 C5
Vicarage Rd *BPR/DUF* DE56 ......12 A2
   MCKLVR DE3 ......39 H4
   MELB/CHEL DE73 ......63 G2
Vicarwood Av *BPR/DUF* DE56 ......12 D3
   DERBYW DE22 ......34 A2
Victor Av *DERBYW* DE22 ......34 A3
Victoria Av *BWSH/BRSTN* DE72 ......45 G4
   BWSH/BRSTN DE72 ......56 C2
Victoria Cl *MCKLVR* DE3 ......40 B2
Victoria Rd *BWSH/BRSTN* DE72 ......56 D2
Victoria St *CDON/KEG* DE74 ......73 E2
   DERBY DE1 ......2 D6
   MELB/CHEL DE73 ......75 H3
Victory Rd *DERBYSE* DE24 ......52 C2
Village St *NORM/LIT* DE23 ......52 A1
Villa St *BWSH/BRSTN* DE72 ......57 E2
Vincent Av *DERBYE* DE21 ......44 D3
Vincent Cl *BPR/DUF* DE56 ......13 H2
Vincent St *NORM/LIT* DE23 ......42 A5
Vine Cl *NORM/LIT* DE23 ......51 C5
Viola Cl *DERBYE* DE21 ......28 B5
Violet St *NORM/LIT* DE23 ......42 A5
Vivian St *DERBYE* DE21 ......34 C3
Vulcan St *NORM/LIT* DE23 ......42 C5

W

Wade Av *NORM/LIT* DE23 ......41 F4
Wadebridge Gv *DERBYSE* DE24 ......54 B4

Wade Dr *MCKLVR* DE3 ......40 B4
Wade St *NORM/LIT* DE23 ......41 F4
Wagtail Cl *DERBYSE* DE24 ......51 G5
Waingroves Rd *RIPLEY* DE5 ......9 G1
Wakami Crs *MELB/CHEL* DE73 ......63 H2
Wakelyn Cl *BWSH/BRSTN* DE72 ......66 C3
Walbrook Rd *NORM/LIT* DE23 ......42 A5
Walcote Cl *BPR/DUF* DE56 ......6 D2
Waldene Dr *DERBYSE* DE24 ......53 H3
Waldorf Av *DERBYSE* DE24 ......53 H2
The Walk *BPR/DUF* DE56 ......14 A2
Walk Cl *BWSH/BRSTN* DE72 ......56 D2
Walker La *DERBY* DE1 ......2 B2
Wallace St *DERBYW* DE22 ......41 F1
Wallfields Cl *RDERBYSW* DE65 ......60 A1
Wallis Cl *BWSH/BRSTN* DE72 ......56 D2
Walnut Av *DERBYSE* DE24 ......54 A2
Walnut Cl *BWSH/BRSTN* DE72 ......65 G4
   MELB/CHEL DE73 ......63 H4
   MELB/CHEL DE73 ......68 B1
   RDERBYSW DE65 ......49 E4
Walnut Rd *BPR/DUF* DE56 ......6 C4
Walnut St *DERBYE* DE24 ......52 D2
Walpole St *DERBYE* DE21 ......3 K1
Walsham Ct *DERBYSE* DE24 ......34 D3
Walter St *BWSH/BRSTN* DE72 ......56 C2
   DERBY DE1 ......33 H4
Waltham Av *DERBYSE* DE24 ......52 A5
Walthamstow Dr *DERBYW* DE22 ......33 E5
Walton Av *DERBYSE* DE24 ......53 F5
Walton Dr *NORM/LIT* DE23 ......51 H2
Walton Hl *CDON/KEG* DE74 ......72 C3
Walton Rd *DERBYE* DE21 ......43 C1
Wansfell Cl *MCKLVR* DE3 ......40 B5
Wardlow Av *NORM/LIT* DE23 ......35 H3
Ward's La *BWSH/BRSTN* DE72 ......57 G1
   MELB/CHEL DE73 ......69 G5
Ward St *DERBYW* DE22 ......41 H2
Wardswood Cl
   BWSH/BRSTN DE72 ......46 A5
Wardwick *DERBY* DE1 ......2 C3
Warner St *DERBYW* DE22 ......42 A3
   MCKLVR DE3 ......40 A5
Warren St *DERBYW* DE22 ......53 C1
Warsick La *MELB/CHEL* DE73 ......74 A2
Warwick Av *NORM/LIT* DE23 ......41 G5
Warwick Gdns *BPR/DUF* DE56 ......7 E2
Warwick St *DERBYSE* DE24 ......43 E4
Washington Av *DERBYE* DE21 ......36 A5
Washington Cl
   MELB/CHEL DE73 ......75 H3
Waterford Dr *DERBYE* DE21 ......43 H2
Watergo La *MCKLVR* DE3 ......49 H4
Watering La *BPR/DUF* DE56 ......13 E4
Waterloo Ct *DERBY* DE1 ......34 C4
The Water Mdw
   MELB/CHEL DE73 ......69 E1
Watermeadow Rd
   DERBYSE DE24 ......53 H4
Waterside Cl *DERBYW* DE22 ......34 B1
Watson St *DERBY* DE1 ......33 H5
Watten Cl *DERBYSE* DE24 ......62 A2
Waveney Cl *DERBYW* DE22 ......26 C3
Waverley St *DERBYSE* DE24 ......52 D2
Waverley Ter *NORM/LIT* * DE23 ......42 B3
Wayfaring Rd *DERBYE* DE21 ......35 H2
Wayzgoose Dr *DERBYE* DE21 ......3 H2
Weavers Cl *BPR/DUF* DE56 ......6 D1
   BWSH/BRSTN DE72 ......46 A5
Webster St *DERBY* DE1 ......2 B6
Weirfield Rd *DERBYW* DE22 ......34 B1
Welbeck Gv *DERBYW* DE22 ......25 G5
Welland Cl *MCKLVR* DE3 ......40 A3
Weldon St *RIPLEY* DE5 ......9 F5
Wellesley Av *NORM/LIT* DE23 ......51 C2
Wellington Ct *BPR/DUF* DE56 ......6 A4
Wellington Crs *DERBY* * DE1 ......3 G6
Wellington St *DERBYE* DE21 ......3 F7
Well La *BPR/DUF* DE56 ......12 A3
Wells Ct *NORM/LIT* * DE23 ......50 B2
Wells Rd *MCKLVR* DE3 ......40 B4
Well St *DERBY* DE1 ......34 B4
Well Yd *BPR/DUF* * DE56 ......6 B2
Welney Cl *MCKLVR* DE3 ......50 A1
Welshpool Rd *DERBYE* DE21 ......35 G2
Welwyn Av *DERBYSE* DE24 ......53 F5
   DERBYW DE22 ......25 G5
Wembley Gdns *DERBYW* DE22 ......32 D5
Wendover Cl *MCKLVR* DE3 ......39 H5
Wenlock Cl *MCKLVR* DE3 ......50 A1
Wensley Dr *DERBYE* DE21 ......45 E3
Wentworth Cl *MCKLVR* DE3 ......40 C5
Werburgh Cl *DERBYE* DE21 ......44 C2
Werburgh St *DERBYW* DE22 ......2 B6
Wesley La *BWSH/BRSTN* DE72 ......45 H1
Wesley Rd *DERBYSE* DE24 ......54 A4
Wessington Ms *DERBYW* DE22 ......33 H2
West Av *BWSH/BRSTN* DE72 ......56 C1

West Bank Av *DERBYW* DE22 ......34 A3
West Bank Rd *DERBYW* DE22 ......33 H3
West Bank Rd *DERBYW* DE22 ......25 H3
Westbourne Pk *DERBYW* DE22 ......32 C5
Westbury Ct *DERBYSE* DE24 ......41 H3
Westbury Gdns *BPR/DUF* DE56 ......6 D2
Westbury St *DERBYW* DE22 ......41 G3
West Cl *DERBYW* DE22 ......33 H1
West Cottages *DERBYE* * DE21 ......43 H4
West Croft Av *NORM/LIT* DE23 ......51 G4
Westdene Av *DERBYSE* DE24 ......53 E4
West Dr *MCKLVR* DE3 ......40 A4
West End Dr *BWSH/BRSTN* DE72 ......66 B3
Western Rd *MCKLVR* DE3 ......40 B4
   NORM/LIT DE23 ......42 A3
Westgreen Av *DERBYSE* DE24 ......53 E4
West Gv *DERBYSE* DE24 ......53 E4
Westhall Rd *MCKLVR* DE3 ......40 A3
West Lawn *RDERBYSW* DE65 ......59 H2
Westleigh Av *DERBYW* DE22 ......33 F5
Westley Crs *DERBYE* DE21 ......19 E3
Westminster St *DERBYSE* DE24 ......53 G1
Westmorland Cl *DERBYE* DE21 ......3 H1
Weston Park Av
   DERBYSE DE24 ......63 E1
Weston Ri *MELB/CHEL* DE73 ......66 B3
Weston Rd *BWSH/BRSTN* DE72 ......71 E1
West Park Rd *DERBYW* DE22 ......33 H3
West Rd *DERBYE* DE21 ......44 C1
West Rw *DERBYW* DE22 ......34 B2
West Service Rd *DERBYE* DE21 ......43 H4
West View Av *NORM/LIT* DE23 ......51 E2
Westwood Dr *DERBYSE* DE24 ......53 E4
Wetherby Rd *DERBYSE* DE24 ......53 E2
Weyacres *BWSH/BRSTN* DE72 ......45 G5
The Wharf *BWSH/BRSTN* DE72 ......66 D3
Wharfedale Cl *DERBYW* DE22 ......26 C4
Wheatcroft Wy *DERBYE* DE21 ......34 D1
Wheathill Gv *NORM/LIT* DE23 ......50 D3
Wheatland Cl *DERBYSE* DE24 ......61 F2
Wheatsheaf Cl *DERBYE* DE21 ......36 B1
Wheeldon Av *BPR/DUF* DE56 ......6 C3
   DERBYW DE22 ......33 H4
Whenby Cl *MCKLVR* DE3 ......39 H4
Whernside Cl *DERBYSE* DE24 ......54 B3
Whilton Ct *BPR/DUF* DE56 ......7 E3
Whinbush Av *DERBYSE* DE24 ......53 F4
Whiston St *NORM/LIT* DE23 ......42 B4
Whitaker Gdns *NORM/LIT* DE23 ......41 H4
Whitaker Rd *NORM/LIT* DE23 ......41 H4
Whitaker St *NORM/LIT* DE23 ......42 B4
Whitby Av *DERBYE* DE21 ......34 D2
Whitecross Gdns *DERBY* DE1 ......33 H4
Whitecross St *DERBY* DE1 ......33 H5
Whitehaven Gv
   MELB/CHEL DE73 ......63 H1
Whitehouse Cl *DERBYSE* DE24 ......53 E5
Whitehouse Ri *BPR/DUF* DE56 ......5 H1
Whitehurst St *DERBYSE* DE24 ......53 E2
White La *BPR/DUF* DE56 ......4 A4
Whitemoor Hall *BPR/DUF* DE56 ......7 E2
Whitemoor La *BPR/DUF* DE56 ......7 E2
White St *DERBYW* DE22 ......33 H1
Whiteway *DERBYW* DE22 ......33 H1
Whitewell Gdns *DERBYSE* DE24 ......54 B4
Whitmore Rd *DERBYE* DE21 ......35 C5
Whitstable Cl *NORM/LIT* DE23 ......51 C5
Whittaker La *DERBYE* DE21 ......19 E3
Whittington St *DERBYSE* DE24 ......53 E4
Whittlebury Dr *NORM/LIT* DE23 ......50 C2
Whyteleafe Gv *DERBYE* DE21 ......36 A2
Wickersley Cl *DERBYW* DE22 ......33 H1
Wicksteed Cl *BPR/DUF* DE56 ......7 E2
Widdybank Cl *DERBYW* DE22 ......33 F1
Wigmore Cl *MCKLVR* DE3 ......39 H3
Wilders Lea Ct *BPR/DUF* DE56 ......6 B5
Wildpark La *ASHB* DE6 ......22 B2
Wildsmith St *DERBYSE* DE24 ......53 H1
Wild St *DERBYW* DE22 ......41 G1
Wilfred St *NORM/LIT* DE24 ......42 C4
Wilkins Dr *DERBYSE* DE24 ......53 F2
Willesden Av *DERBYW* DE22 ......32 D4
Willetts Rd *DERBYE* DE21 ......35 H4
William St *BPR/DUF* DE56 ......6 A3
   DERBY DE1 ......33 H4
Willington Rd *RDERBYSW* DE65 ......48 B5
   RDERBYSW DE65 ......59 H4
Wilin St *NORM/LIT* DE23 ......42 A5
Willoughby Ct
   BWSH/BRSTN * DE72 ......47 G2
Willowbrook Gra
   MELB/CHEL DE73 ......63 H4
Willow Cl *BWSH/BRSTN* DE72 ......65 G5
   DERBYW DE22 ......34 A1
Willow Cft *DERBYSE* DE24 ......54 B5
Willowcroft Rd *DERBYE* DE21 ......44 C3

Willow Gv *BPR/DUF* DE56 ......6 B
Willowherb Cl *DERBYSE* DE24 ......62 A
Willow Park Wy
   BWSH/BRSTN DE72 ......65 F
Willow Rd *CDON/KEG* DE74 ......73 E
Willow Rw *DERBY* DE1 ......2 B
Willowsend Cl *RDERBYSW* DE65 ......60 A
Willson Av *NORM/LIT* DE23 ......51 F
Willson Rd *NORM/LIT* DE23 ......51 F
Wilmington Av *DERBYSE* DE24 ......54 A
Wilmore Rd *DERBYSE* DE24 ......52 C
Wilmot Av *BWSH/BRSTN* DE72 ......70 D
   DERBYE DE21 ......43 G
Wilmot Dr *ILK* DE7 ......15 E
Wilmot Rd *BPR/DUF* DE56 ......6 B
Wilmot St *DERBY* DE1 ......2 D
Wilmslow Dr *DERBYE* DE21 ......36 A
Wilne La *BWSH/BRSTN* DE72 ......57 F
   BWSH/BRSTN DE72 ......67 E
Wilne Rd *BWSH/BRSTN* DE72 ......56 D
Wilson Av *HEANOR* DE75 ......9 G
Wilson Cl *MCKLVR* DE3 ......49 H
Wilson Ri *MELB/CHEL* DE73 ......76 D
Wilson Rd *DERBYE* DE21 ......35 G
Wilson St *DERBY* DE1 ......2 B
Wilsthorpe Rd
   BWSH/BRSTN DE72 ......57 H
   DERBYE DE21 ......35 G
Wilton Cl *DERBYSE* DE24 ......61 F
Wiltshire Rd *DERBYE* DE21 ......35 E
Wimbledon Rd *DERBYW* DE22 ......32 D
Wimbourne Cl
   MELB/CHEL DE73 ......63 H
Wimpole Gdns *DERBYW* DE22 ......33 E
Wincanton Cl *DERBYSE* DE24 ......43 E
Winchcombe Wy *DERBYE* DE21 ......35 H
Winchester Crs *DERBYE* DE21 ......35 E
Windermere Crs *DERBYW* DE22 ......25 H
Windermere Dr *DERBYE* DE21 ......44 D
Windley Crs *DERBYW* DE22 ......34 A
Windley La *BPR/DUF* DE56 ......10 B
Windmill Av *BPR/DUF* DE56 ......14 A
Windmill Cl *BWSH/BRSTN* DE72 ......45 H
   CDON/KEG DE74 ......73 E
   DERBYSE DE24 ......54 C
Windmill Cottages
   DERBYE * DE21 ......27 G
Windmill Hill La *DERBYW* DE22 ......33 F
Windmill La *BPR/DUF* DE56 ......6 B
Windmill Ri *BPR/DUF* DE56 ......6 B
Windmill Rd *RDERBYSW* DE65 ......58 A
Windrush Cl *DERBYW* DE22 ......26 C
Windsor Av *MELB/CHEL* DE73 ......75 H
   NORM/LIT DE23 ......51 E
Windsor Cl *BWSH/BRSTN* DE72 ......45 H
Windsor Ct *MCKLVR* DE3 ......40 A
Windsor Dr *DERBYE* DE21 ......37 E
Windy La *DERBYE* DE21 ......18 D
Wingerworth Park Rd
   DERBYE DE21 ......44 D
Wingfield Dr *DERBYSE* DE24 ......53 G
Winslow Gn *DERBYE* DE21 ......36 A
Winster Cl *BPR/DUF* DE56 ......6 C
Winster Rd *DERBYE* DE21 ......35 F
Wintergreen Dr *NORM/LIT* DE23 ......50 C
Wirksworth Rd *BPR/DUF* DE56 ......10 B
   BPR/DUF DE56 ......17 G
Wisgreaves Rd *DERBYSE* DE24 ......53 G
Witham Dr *NORM/LIT* DE23 ......51 G
Witney Cl *DERBYSE* DE24 ......52 D
Witton Ct *DERBYW* DE22 ......51 G
Woburn Pl *DERBYW* DE22 ......41 E
Wolfa St *DERBYW* DE22 ......2 A
Wollaton Rd *DERBYE* DE21 ......35 G
Wolverley Gra *DERBYSE* DE24 ......54 C
Woodale Cl *NORM/LIT* DE23 ......50 C
Woodbridge Cl *MELB/CHEL* DE73 ......63 G
Woodchester Dr *DERBYSE* DE24 ......54 C
Wood Close Camp *DERBYE* DE21 ......26 D
Woodcote Wy *NORM/LIT* DE23 ......50 D
Wood Cft *NORM/LIT* DE23 ......51 G
Woodfall La *DERBYW* DE22 ......16 C
Woodford Rd *DERBYW* DE22 ......32 D
Woodgate Dr
   MELB/CHEL DE73 ......63 H
Woodhall Dr *NORM/LIT* DE23 ......50 B
Woodhouse Rd *BPR/DUF* DE56 ......13 H
Woodhurst Cl *DERBYE* DE21 ......35 E
Woodland Av
   BWSH/BRSTN DE72 ......45 H
Woodland Rd *DERBYW* DE22 ......33 H
The Woodlands
   MELB/CHEL DE73 ......76 A
Woodlands Av *DERBYSE* DE24 ......53 F
Woodlands Cl *DERBYE* DE21 ......18 C
   MELB/CHEL DE73 ......75 H
Woodlands La *DERBYW* DE22 ......25 G
   MELB/CHEL DE73 ......63 H

Index - featured places

Kingsway Hospital
DERBYW DE22 .... 41 E2
Kingsway Hospital
School of Nursing
DERBYW DE22 .... 41 E2
Kingsway Industrial Park
DERBYW DE22 .... 41 E1
Kingsway Retail Park
DERBYW DE22 .... 41 F1
Kirk Langley CE Primary School
ASHB DE6 .... 31 E1
Ladylea Industrial Estate
ILK DE7 .... 14 A3
Lancaster Sports Centre
DERBY DE1 .... 2 C2
Landau Forte College City
Technical College
DERBY DE1 .... 2 D1
Lawn Primary School
DERBYW DE22 .... 33 G2
Lees Brook Community School
DERBYE DE21 .... 36 A3
Little Eaton Primary School
DERBYE DE21 .... 26 D1
Littleover Community School
NORM/LIT DE23 .... 50 C1
Littleover Medical Centre
NORM/LIT DE23 .... 41 E5
Long Row Primary School
BPR/DUF DE56 .... 6 A3
Loscoe CE Primary School
HEANOR DE75 .... 9 G3
Lum Farm Leisure Centre
RIPLEY DE5 .... 8 D2
Mackworth College
DERBYW DE22 .... 40 C1
Main Shopping Centre
DERBY DE1 .... 2 E5
Markeaton Crematorium
DERBYW DE22 .... 33 E4
Markeaton Primary School
DERBYW DE22 .... 33 H4
Meadow Farm Primary School
DERBYE DE21 .... 43 H2
The Meadows Industrial Estate
DERBYE DE21 .... 3 G3
The Meadows Primary School
BPR/DUF DE56 .... 17 G2
Melbourne Halland Gardens
MELB/CHEL DE73 .... 76 B3
Melbourne J & I School
MELB/CHEL DE73 .... 76 A2
Merrill College
DERBYSE DE24 .... 53 F3
Meteor Business Park
DERBY DE1 .... 34 C4
Metro Cinema
DERBY DE1 .... 2 C5
Mickleover Golf Club
NORM/LIT DE23 .... 40 C5
Mickleover Primary School
MCKLVR DE3 .... 40 A4
Mickleover Surgery
MCKLVR DE3 .... 40 B5
Milford Primary School
BPR/DUF DE56 .... 12 B3
Millennium Business Centre
DERBYE DE21 .... 43 F2
The Moore Clinic
BPR/DUF DE56 .... 6 A3
Moorhead Primary School
DERBYSE DE24 .... 53 G3
Moorways Sports Centre
DERBYSE DE24 .... 52 D3
Moorways Stadium
DERBYSE DE24 .... 53 E3
Morley Hayes Golf Club
ILK DE7 .... 20 D4
Morley Primary School
ILK DE7 .... 28 B1

Murray Park Community School
MCKLVR DE3 .... 40 C2
Newchase Business Park
DERBYSE DE24 .... 42 D5
Nightingale Business Park
DERBYSE DE24 .... 53 E1
Nightingale Infant School
DERBYSE DE24 .... 52 D2
Nightingale Junior School
DERBYSE DE24 .... 52 D1
Noel Baker Community School
DERBYSE DE24 .... 53 G5
Normanton Junior School
NORM/LIT DE23 .... 51 H2
Normanton Village
Infant School
NORM/LIT DE23 .... 52 A2
Oakwood Infant School
DERBYSE DE24 .... 53 H3
Oakwood Junior School
DERBYSE DE24 .... 53 H3
Oakwood Leisure Centre
DERBYE DE21 .... 35 H1
Oakwood Medical Centre
DERBYE DE21 .... 35 H2
Ockbrook School
BWSH/BRSTN DE72 .... 45 H1
Old Hall Mill Business Park
DERBYE DE21 .... 26 D1
The Old Vicarage School
DERBYW DE22 .... 34 B1
Orchard Primary School
CDON/KEG DE74 .... 72 D3
Osmaston Park
Industrial Estate
DERBYSE DE24 .... 43 E5
DERBYSE DE24 .... 53 F1
Parker Industrial Estate
DERBY DE1 .... 34 C3
Park Farm Medical Centre
DERBYW DE22 .... 33 G1
Parkview Primary School
DERBYE DE21 .... 35 H1
Peartree Clinic
NORM/LIT DE23 .... 42 B5
Pear Tree Infant School
NORM/LIT DE23 .... 42 B5
Pear Tree Medical Centre
NORM/LIT DE23 .... 42 B5
Perkins Industrial Estate
DERBYE DE21 .... 34 D3
Peter Baines Industrial Estate
DERBYW DE22 .... 2 B6
Pickfords House Museum of
Georgian Life & Costume
DERBY DE1 .... 2 A3
Police Museum
DERBY DE1 .... 2 C2
Portway Infant School
DERBYW DE22 .... 25 H4
Portway Junior School
DERBYW DE22 .... 25 H4
Pottery Primary School
BPR/DUF DE56 .... 6 D3
Prime Industrial Estate
NORM/LIT DE23 .... 42 D4
Queen St Baths
DERBY DE1 .... 2 C2
Queens Leisure Centre
DERBY DE1 .... 2 C2
Racecourse Industrial Estate
DERBYE DE21 .... 34 D3
Ravensdale Infant School
MCKLVR DE3 .... 40 B3
Redhill Primary School
BWSH/BRSTN DE72 .... 46 A1
Redwood J & I School
DERBYSE DE24 .... 61 H1
Reigate Primary School
DERBYW DE22 .... 32 C4

Richardson Endowed
Primary School
ILK DE7 .... 15 E4
Ridgeway Infant School
NORM/LIT DE23 .... 51 G2
Risley Lower Grammar CE
Primary School
BWSH/BRSTN DE72 .... 47 H2
Riversdale Surgery
BPR/DUF DE56 .... 6 A3
Robinsons Industrial Estate
NORM/LIT DE23 .... 42 D4
Roehill Infant School
NORM/LIT DE23 .... 42 C3
Rosehill Business Centre
NORM/LIT DE23 .... 42 B4
Royal Crown Derby
Visitor Centre
NORM/LIT DE23 .... 42 C3
Royal School for the Deaf
DERBYW DE22 .... 33 G5
RTC Business Park
DERBYE DE21 .... 52 C1
St Albans RC Primary School
DERBYE DE21 .... 35 G5
St Andrews CE Primary School
ILK DE7 .... 29 G3
St Andrews Special School
DERBYE DE21 .... 35 F1
St Benedict RC School
DERBYW DE22 .... 34 A2
St Chadsce Infant School
NORM/LIT DE23 .... 42 A3
St Clares Special School
MCKLVR DE3 .... 40 C4
St Edwards CE Primary School
CDON/KEG DE74 .... 73 E4
St Elizabeths RC
Primary School
BPR/DUF DE56 .... 6 A2
St Georges Catholic
Primary School
NORM/LIT DE23 .... 51 F2
St Giles Special School
DERBYE DE21 .... 34 D2
St Helens Business Centre
DERBY DE1 .... 2 B1
St James CE Infant School
NORM/LIT DE23 .... 2 E7
St John Fisher RC
Primary School
DERBYSE DE24 .... 54 B1
St Johns CE Primary School
BPR/DUF DE56 .... 6 B2
St Josephs RC Primary School
NORM/LIT DE23 .... 2 B7
St Marys RC Primary School
DERBY DE1 .... 2 C1
St Peters CE Junior School
NORM/LIT DE23 .... 41 E5
St Werburghs CE
Primary School
DERBYE DE21 .... 44 C1
Sale & Davys CE
Primary School
MELB/CHEL DE73 .... 68 B2
Shardlow Business Park
BWSH/BRSTN DE72 .... 66 A3
Shardlow Marina Caravan Park
BWSH/BRSTN DE72 .... 67 E3
Shardlow Primary School
BWSH/BRSTN DE72 .... 66 B3
Sherwin Sports Centre
NORM/LIT DE23 .... 52 C1
Showcase Cinemas
NORM/LIT DE23 .... 52 B2
Sidney Robinson Business Park
DERBYSE DE24 .... 43 E5
Silverhill Primary School
MCKLVR DE3 .... 39 H3

Sinfin Central Business Park
DERBYSE DE24 .... 62 A
Sinfin Community School
DERBYSE DE24 .... 61 H
Sinfin Golf Club
DERBYSE DE24 .... 52 B
Sinfin Primary School
DERBYSE DE24 .... 52 A
Sir Francis Ley Industrial Park
NORM/LIT DE23 .... 42 D
Southgate Infant School
DERBYSE DE24 .... 53 C
Southgate Retail Park
NORM/LIT DE23 .... 42 A
Springfield Primary School
DERBYE DE21 .... 44 C
Stadium Business Court
DERBYSE DE24 .... 53 F
Stanley Common CE
Primary School
ILK DE7 .... 21 G
Stenson Fields Primary School
DERBYSE DE24 .... 61 G
Street Lane Primary School
RIPLEY DE5 .... 8 A
Sunney Hill Infant School
NORM/LIT DE23 .... 51 H
Swarkestone Boat Club
MELB/CHEL DE73 .... 69 E
Temple House Clinic
NORM/LIT DE23 .... 2 C
Thornhill Day Hospital
DERBYW DE22 .... 41 E
Tomlinson Industrial Estate
DERBYE DE21 .... 34 C
Trent Lane Industrial Estate
CDON/KEG DE74 .... 73 E
UCI Cinemas
DERBYE DE21 .... 34 D
University of Derby
DERBY DE1 .... 2 A
DERBYW DE22 .... 33 G
DERBYW DE22 .... 41 G
MCKLVR DE3 .... 40 C
Victorian Market Hall
DERBY DE1 .... 2 D
Vidya Medical Centre
DERBY DE1 .... 2 D
Virgin Active - Derby
DERBYE DE21 .... 3 G
Walter Evans CE
Primary School
DERBYW DE22 .... 34 A
Waverley Street Clinic
DERBYSE DE24 .... 52 D
Wellside Medical Centre
DERBY DE1 .... 2 C
West Park Community School
DERBYE DE21 .... 44 C
William Gilbert Endowed
Primary School
BPR/DUF DE56 .... 17 H
Willow Farm Business Park
CDON/KEG DE74 .... 73 E
Willow Sports Centre
DERBY DE1 .... 2 B
Wilmorton Community
Primary School
DERBYSE DE24 .... 43 E
Woodlands Community School
DERBYW DE22 .... 25 G
Wren Park Primary School
MCKLVR DE3 .... 40 D
Wyvern Business Park
DERBYE DE21 .... 43 H